FRANZ KAFKA AND PRAGUE

A LITERARY GUIDE
BY HARALD SALFELLNER

VITALIS

BIOGRAPHICAL OVERVIEW

JULY 3, 1883:
Franz Kafka is born in Prague, the first son of the merchant Hermann Kafka and his wife Julie, née Löwy. The Kafkas have two other sons who die in infancy; three sisters are born close together: Gabriele (Elli), Valerie (Valli), and Ottilie (Ottla).

SEPTEMBER 1889 TO SUMMER 1893:
Kafka attends the German State Primary School for Boys at the Fleischmarkt (Meat Market).

SEPTEMBER 1893 TO JULY 1901:
Kafka attends the k. u. k. (Imperial and Royal) State German-Language Secondary School in the Kinsky Palace on the Old Town Square.

Franz Kafka (1906).

JUNE 13, 1896:
Bar-Mitzvah.

MAY TO JULY 1901:
Written and oral final exams for the leaving certificate at the German State Secondary School.

OCTOBER 1, 1901:
Beginning of studies at the k. k. (Imperial, Royal) German Karl-Ferdinand University in Prague (initially two weeks of chemistry, followed by lectures in law, history of art, philosophy, and German studies, and finally, from the winter semester 1902/03, jurisprudence).

OCTOBER 23, 1902:
First meeting with Max Brod; start of their life-long friendship.

JUNE 18, 1906:
Graduation as Doctor of Law from the Karl-Ferdinand University.

PRESUMABLY FROM FALL 1906 ON:
The first version of *Wedding Preparations in the Country (Hochzeitsvorbereitungen auf dem Lande)* is written. In summer 1909 Kafka writes two more versions of the novella.

OCTOBER 1906:
Beginning of one-year internship at court, at first at the State Civil Court on the Obstmarkt (Fruit Market), after six months at the criminal court on the Karlsplatz (Charles Square).

OCTOBER 1, 1907:
Kafka begins a job as an assistant in the private insurance company "Assicurazioni Generali" on Wenceslas Square.

2

CURRICULUM VITÆ.

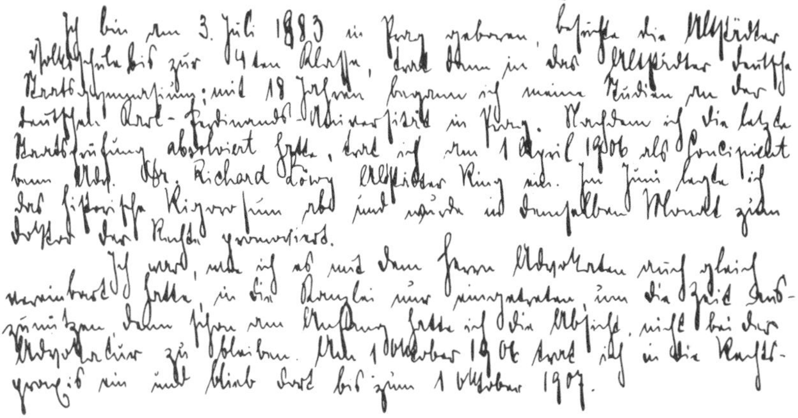

[Handwritten text in German cursive]

MARCH 1908:
First publication of eight prose texts in the magazine *Hyperion*.

JULY 30, 1908:
Kafka is given a position as an assistant official in the semi-governmental "Workers' Accident Insurance Company for the Kingdom of Bohemia". In the course of the years to come he will be promoted to head-clerk.

WINTER 1911/12:
The first draft of the America-novel, *The Man Who Disappeared (Der Verschollene)*, is written.

JANUARY 1, 1912:
Official founding of the "Prague Asbestos Works Hermann & Co." ("Prager Asbestwerke Hermann & Co."), a company in which Kafka is made a partner with his father's money.

AUGUST 13, 1912:
Kafka makes the acquaintance of Felice Bauer, who is employed in a sales company in Berlin. On September 20 he writes the first of numerous letters to her.

SEPTEMBER 22/23, 1912:
In one night Kafka writes the story *The Judgment (Das Urteil)*.

NOVEMBER 17 TO DECEMBER 6, 1912:
The Metamorphosis (Die Verwandlung) is

Max Brod (around 1900).

3

Franz Kafka (1917).

written. The story is published in October 1915 in the journal *Die Weißen Blätter (The White Pages)*.

DECEMBER 1912:
The collection *Meditation (Betrachtung)*, Kafka's first book, is published by Ernst Rowohlt in Leipzig.

JUNE 1, 1914:
Official engagement to Felice Bauer in Berlin. Due to Kafka's doubts, the engagement is called off following a meeting in the Hotel "Askanischer Hof" on July 12, 1914.

AUGUST 1914:
Start of work on *The Trial (Der Prozeß)*. In January 1915 Kafka stops work on the unfinished novel.

FROM NOVEMBER 1916 ON:
Kafka uses the small house in Alchemists' Lane in the Hradschin (Prague Castle complex), rented by his sister Ottla, to write. Here he writes, among other texts, the stories

that will appear in the collection *A Country Doctor (Ein Landarzt)*, published by Kurt Wolff in April / May 1920.

BEGINNING OF JULY 1917:
Second engagement to Felice Bauer in Prague. The engagement is called off again on December 25.

AUGUST 12/13, 1917:
Kafka suffers a hemorrhage during the night. On September 3 a doctor he consults diagnoses "catarrh of the outer lobes of the lung".

JANUARY 22, 1919:
First meeting with Julie Wohryzek while recuperating in Schelesen. They get engaged, probably in September, but terminate the engagement a few weeks later.

NOVEMBER 1919:
In Schelesen Kafka writes his *Letter to Father (Brief an den Vater)* – over one hundred pages.

Milena Jesenská with her tennis coach (1911).

AROUND APRIL 8, 1920:
Beginning of his correspondence with the journalist Milena Jesenská. This correspondence soon develops into a love affair with the young married Czech woman.

END OF JANUARY 1922:
Kafka begins work on his last novel *The Castle* (*Das Schloß*). He abandons it at the end of August and the unfinished work is only published posthumously by Max Brod.

JULY 1, 1922:
Since there is no hope for Kafka's recovery in the near future, he applies for and is granted early retirement.

JULY 1923:
Journey to the Baltic Sea resort of Müritz, where Kafka meets Dora Diamant. He begins a love affair with the young Jewish girl from Eastern Europe.

Dora Diamant in a passport photograph (1928).

Sanatorium Hoffmann in Kierling.

SEPTEMBER 24, 1923:
Kafka leaves Prague and moves in with Dora Diamant in Berlin.

MARCH 17, 1924:
After a rapid decline in the state of his health, Kafka returns to Prague and stays for several weeks with his parents in the Oppelt-House.

APRIL 1924:
Kafka's tuberculosis has attacked his larynx. In winter clothes Kafka only weighs 49 kg.

APRIL 19, 1924:
After staying in the Wienerwald Sanatorium in Lower Austria and attempted treatment at Professor Dr Markus Hajek's Laryngological Clinic in Vienna, Kafka is admitted to the "Sanatorium Dr Hoffmann" in Kierling near Klosterneuburg.

JUNE 3, 1924:
Kafka dies in the Sanatorium in Kierling, cared for to the end by his lover Dora Diamant and by his friend, the physician Robert Klopstock. His remains are returned to Prague by train. Kafka's burial at the New Jewish Cemetery in Prague on June 11 is attended by his friends and family, and also by many German and Czech lovers of literature.

5

Franz Kafka's Prague

Let us abandon the romantic notion that Kafka's Prague was a quaint little city in the provinces of the old Austrian monarchy. Long before the Hapsburgs came to power in Bohemia, the cultural and political influence of Prague was felt far beyond its national borders. The Bohemian capital frequently took center stage in European history, becoming the intellectual focal point of the continent. Situated at the crossroads of important trade routes, the city was of considerable strategic importance, both as a bridge to the East, which it has remained to this day, and as a political and cultural link between the old Austria and the up-and-coming metropolis of Berlin in the late 19th century. The new European roles to be played by Prussia and Austria were allocated on the battlefield of Königgrätz in 1866 and the outcome was established in the "Peace of Prague", a deeply symbolic act for that city.

Prague's coat of arms.

Since its foundation in the 9th century, Prague has been the capital of the Czech people. However, it always maintained a special significance as the center of the economically vital regions of German-speaking Bohemia, surrounding the predominantly Slavic core of Inner Bohemia. The capital linked such disparate regions as the barren Giant Mountains (Riesengebirge) and the industrial areas of northern Bohemia with the farms of the Egerland and the romantic Bohemian Forest, beloved of the mid-19th century German author Adalbert Stifter.

Despite this topographically central position and its obvious bridging function, Prague had been forced to give way to Imperial Vienna in the diplomatic concert of central Europe in the 18th and 19th centuries. During Kafka's lifetime, however, things began to shift again. There were stormy developments in almost every area of metropolitan life; both old sections of the city and the new suburbs were in

Left: Franz Kafka in front of the Oppelt-House (1922).

7

a violent state of ferment. The population grew rapidly and soon spread beyond the historical boundaries of the city.

With a good deal of unease, the German patrician class living in the better quarters of the city found themselves face to face with an ever increasing Czech suburban proletariat. By the 19th century, the Prague German community, once the backbone of the influential bourgeois society and of the ruling administration, was increasingly outnumbered and marginalized, leading to a perceptible loss of influence and political power. In the 1840s there was still a German majority in Prague, but in the year of Kafka's birth the numbers had undergone a dramatic reversal. In 1880 about 32,000 Prague Germans confronted 126,000 Czechs. The consequences were obvious: by as early as 1882 not one German councilor had a seat in the town hall; from 1883 on there was also a Czech majority in parliament. Wherever possible, war was declared on everything German and the Czech language was given preference. Thus, from 1891 on German street signs were removed. In the streets and squares, Czech national symbols were put up and, if possible, the corresponding German ones taken away. In a tenacious struggle the Czechs succeeded in "retaking" their city sign by sign, monument by monument. Venerable old street names were changed in the new national-political spirit: the old Spornergasse (Spurmakers' Lane) in the Lesser Town (Kleinseite), for example, where the poet Jan Neruda lived, was now to be called Nerudova. This was more than just an act of homage to the great poet – it also hid a full measure of national-political calculation. After the forfeiture of their political power in the city's representative councils, the Germans were more or less forced to suffer these pinprick tactics. Their influence in the National

A Czech street sign on the Lesser Town Square covers up the original bilingual inscription, demonstrating the now Slavic character of the city (around 1912).

Representative Assembly in Vienna ended at the gates of Prague.

Admittedly, the approximately 30,000 to 35,000 Germans, mainly living in the city center at the turn of the 20th century, who now only made up about 7% of the total population, still formed a self-assured and proud upper class, predominantly well-off and frequently outright rich, a city bourgeoisie ensconced in its magnificent villas and patrician apartments enjoying its material possessions and social status. These were the mine owners, the bank directors and businessmen, members of the Bohemian Legislative Assembly, factory owners and university administrators, chief inspectors, and widows of k. k. (imperial, royal) court counselors. This select group was served by two thriving theaters, a university, a technical university, a concert hall, as well as half a dozen German high schools, several prolific German publishing houses, about 200 German societies and clubs ensconced in the so-called German House (Deutsches Haus), and a number of significant German daily papers, among them the *Bohemia*, the *Deutsches Abendblatt*, the *Montagsblatt aus Böhmen*, the official government paper

Only two things are obligatory: don't flirt with Slav society and no inimical behavior toward Jews. Both are principles of existence in the German society here [in Prague].

Friedrich Jodl

9

Prager Abendblatt, the *Union,* which was a Czech paper printed in German, and above all the *Prager Tagblatt,* which in it's heyday appeared in two editions, one in the morning and one in the evening. All those things, of course, were the relics of a once unchallenged cultural dominance, stubbornly paraded like a threatened flag in a sea of Czech pennants. German Prague, unable to recognize its own anachronistic dream world, gave itself up to a late bloom nourished by a great past. Thus, the majority of Germans and Jews lived less in what has often been described as a ghetto, than in an elite ivory tower with little connection to reality.

The epoch of the so-called "Gründerzeit" (the "Foundation Era") and the results of industrialization became evermore apparent in the cityscape. Hundreds of houses, often with a history extending back into the Middle Ages, had to make way for new building projects. Technical innovation and a modernization craze so altered the appearance of many streets that they became unrecognizable. In November 1885, a new water department took up regular operation in the quarter of the city known as Podolí. Now the households in the city could be supplied with drinking water and equipped with English water

National symbols put their stamp on everday life: Seal of the "German Section of the Cultural County Council for the Kingdom of Bohemia" (around 1901).

closets. One by one, the familiar old wells in the small streets of Prague, fashioned out of stone or wood, disappeared from the scene. Architects earned their place in the history of the city with magnificent, showy buildings which demand admiration even today. On the Vyšehrad, the cathedral of Ss Peter and Paul was rebuilt in the Neo-Gothic style (1885–1887), at the upper end of Wenceslas Square the Neo-Renaissance building of the National Museum was constructed (1885–1890) and only a few hundred meters further, the Viennese theater architects Fellner and Helmer erected the New German Theater (1886–1887). In the year 1888 the city bought up the old military fortification walls and trenches between the districts of the Prague New Town (Prager Neustadt) and the Royal Vineyards (Königliche Weinberge). The old walls were torn down, the land was divided into building plots, and the two previously distinct districts could now grow together. From 1891 on, a cable car led up the Laurenziberg, and people on day-excursions could now travel comfortably up to the new observation tower, a very recent addition to the many hundred towers of the Prague landscape. From the top the transformation of the city was obvious: new bridges

Panoramic view of Prague: To the left Prague Castle with the Hradschin and St Vitus' Cathedral, below the Lesser Town with St Nicholas' Cathedral. In the center is Charles Bridge and to the right, on the Moldau riverbank, the Czech National Theater (around 1901).

Prague doesn't let go (…). This little mother has claws. Either you comply or –. We'd have to torch it on two sides, on Vyšehrad and on the Hradschin, to possibly get away.

Franz Kafka
to Oskar Pollak on
December 20, 1902.

11

and elegant town houses, new museums and monuments, here a new civic building, there a modern town hall – wherever Kafka looked, new structures mushroomed on old city grounds imbued with history.

In the Old Town, too, much was built and much was altered. The old Jewish Quarter, which extended out behind the Old Town Square, was especially hard hit by this euphoria for progress. The distinguished Jewish families who had gained wealth in commerce, industry, and administration, had moved out as soon as they were allowed to leave the ghetto. However, those who had stumbled and fallen in society, those with few means and the outright poor still endured life there among prostitutes, crooks, and riffraff who shied away from daylight. Smoky dives, seedy bordellos, lice-infested shelters – this dubious quarter was avoided whenever possible. An average of 1800 inhabitants thronged together per square kilometer – almost three times as many as in the neighboring districts of the Old Town. In the suburbs it probably would not have bothered anyone, but here in the Old Town, in one of the best locations, it did – in short, the old Jewish Quarter stood on very valuable building land. And who would have dared object to the plan of a thorough urban renewal aiming to put an end to the unacceptably unhygienic conditions, breeding grounds for illnesses, even epidemics and pestilence, and which would transform the overpopulated poor quarter into a clean neighborhood with modern palatial apartment houses and elegant Art Nouveau dwellings?

Contemporary literature, too, went through a stormy development. Although out in the rural-industrial fringes of German Bohemia, readers still preferred the diverse literary products of a multiplicity of parochial folk-writers, the literary circles of the capital, especially the urban writers themselves, were finely attuned to new directions in style. There

was no more talk of naturalistic reality, but of Symbolism and Neo-Romanticism, of Impressionism and Expressionism – modern times broke an ever-changing variation of new paths, and the cosmopolitan atmosphere in the city assisted the process. As impenetrable as the conglomeration of political and aesthetic directions was, so numerous and various were the German writers and poets in the shadow of the Hradschin (Prague Castle) who subscribed to them: the lawyer Friedrich Adler, the physician Hugo Salus, the fervently German ballad singer Oskar Wiener, the cosmopolitan poet Rainer Maria Rilke, the "racing reporter" Egon Erwin Kisch, the uncrowned king of the Prague bohème Paul Leppin, and at the head of them all the authors of the so-called "Prague Circle", who had found their home in the city's coffee houses: Franz Werfel, Max Brod, Felix Weltsch, Oskar Baum, Ludwig Winder, and – Franz Kafka. In this cultural golden age, the city could shine as a metropolis alongside such cities as Paris, Berlin, and Vienna, and its exotic character as a city of two nationalities meant that it could claim a position of distinct individuality.

The dark corners, the secretive passages, the dirty, impenetrable windows, dingy courtyards, noisy pubs, and closed taverns still live within us. We walk through the wide streets of the newly built city. Yet our steps and glances are unsure. Inwardly we still tremble as we did in the old narrow streets of misery. Our hearts still do not sense anything of the renewal which was carried out. The unhealthy Jewish ghetto is more palpable in us than the hygienic new city around us. Awake, we are wandering through a dream, we ourselves just specters of times past.

Franz Kafka

The exhibition grounds in the Arboretum (around 1900).

A cleaning unit of the Prague Tramway Service (around 1900).

The ever-present change and progress of civilization was not confined merely to aesthetic questions, to art and culture, rather, it touched all areas of daily life. Commerce, industry, and technology experienced an unimaginable boom. Communication by telephone spread rapidly (from as early as 1889, one could already make long distance calls to Vienna), electricity works enabled the use of newfangled equipment, the Moldau was made navigable, and from the 1890s "die Elektrische", that is, the electric streetcar, and the first motorcars gave a foretaste of a not too far distant transportation revolution. After 1891, the first electric streetcar rumbled through the city, supplied with electricity from a provisional power plant. The route of this "tramway" led from the Belvedere Heights (Letná) out to the Anniversary Exhibition grounds in the Arboretum (Baumgarten); later the tracks were extended to the viceroy's official residential villa, until, in the year 1900, the service was discontinued for financial reasons. In 1894, the first districts of Prague received electric lighting from a small power plant. In the following year, 1895, the first full-scale electric plant in Bohemia was put into operation, the Municipal Electric Works in Prague-Žižkov, and finally, in 1899, the Central Electricity Works of Prague in

Holešovice came on-line. It had been made possible through the combined efforts of a number of leading industrial enterprises. Technological progress was the magic word and new achievements came on the scene at ever shorter intervals, being presented in the newspapers. By 1906 there were already 69 officially registered motorcars zipping around Prague, the first flying machines in which rash young men winged their way upwards into the white clouds appeared on the horizon, and in dark projection rooms the animated pictures of cinematography provided a new view of the great wide world. Beginning in 1907, Prague had its first permanent cinema house, the Biograph Ponrepo in the house "Of the Blue Pike" ("Zum Blauen Hecht") in the Old Town at 20 Karlsgasse (Charles Lane) (I–180). By the time the Great War broke out in 1914, no fewer than 39 movie houses had been established, and inhabitants of Prague could select from the increasingly wide variety of films on offer. Admittedly they showed not much more than theater performances or traditional music hall pieces relatively crudely captured on celluloid, and even those were in black and white, accompanied by only a little live music, but that did not dampen the enthusiasm. Spellbound, Kafka and his friends followed the moving pictures in the "motion picture theaters".

A Benz automobile driving on the ramp leading up to Prague Castle (1898).

Top: An advertisement for the western "Slaves of Gold" that Kafka saw in the Grand Theatre Bio "Elite" (1913).

Bottom right: Poster of the Czech-Slav Folkloristic Exhibition in Prague (1895).

Germans and Jews: for Czech Prague that was at that time almost synonymous and both, Germans and Jews, were equally hated. The Jews spoke German and were Austrian patriots …

Willy Haas

How the city blossomed thanks to the blessings of progress! Everything appeared to become bigger and better, more elegant and richer. To be sure, one had to avoid close examination of the workers' quarters where an explosive mixture of misery and bitterness was brewing, a smoldering social fire, only damped with great effort by laws and decrees. Behind their heavy brocade curtains members of middle class society shook their heads disapprovingly at the new catchwords: workers' movement, universal suffrage, socialism, unions, right to strike, shorter working week – where would it all end? Disputes over small matters here and there were soon followed by strikes and mass demonstrations about greater issues. Today it might be the industrial bakers who poured onto the streets to press for shorter working hours, tomorrow it would be the workers in the laundry business demanding increased pay, and hardly had the striking Smíchov weavers been quelled when the *Prager Tagblatt* reported on demonstrations on Wenceslas Square calling for universal suffrage. The social tensions bore an unmistakable national character – here, the overwhelming majority of the progressive Czechs, there the dark reactionary forces, the Germans, the monarchy, the Jews! While the members of the Sokol movement paraded in the Slavic national colors on the left side of the street, the "buršáci", the derogatory Czech name for members of such German student fraternities (Burschenschaften) as the "Germania", marched stubbornly and defiantly on the right. And in the middle, almost helpless, rode the mounted k. u. k. (imperial and royal) police with truncheons and feathered helmets. Thus, the national conflicts between Czechs and Germans, rooted in the deep past, were swept acrimoniously onto the streets of Prague. Coexistence was increasingly difficult, and the efforts of a minority of clear-thinking individuals were spurned in the face of a majority that did not want to have anything to do with "equalization" of nationalities. Even before the turn of the century, the German-Czech rivalry had matured into a genuine war of attrition in which the rare words of reason and moderation were drowned by the constant screaming of militant radicals on both sides.

At the beginning of the 19th century, the awakening of Czech national consciousness had depended on the work of Czech scholars who wrote their works in German and who were thoroughly familiar with German culture. One need only think of the critic of language and literature Josef Dobrovský, or the conservative nationalist historian František Palacký. How different the situation looked only a few decades later! Radical nationalistic forces steered a course toward confrontation, the clash could not fail to occur sooner or later. The reaction to the language decrees of the former viceroy of Galicia Count Kazimierz Badeni, who in 1895 had been entrusted by Emperor Franz Joseph with the formation of a "strong-handed government", was evidence that any basis of discussion between the two national entities in Bohemia had long since been lost. Badeni wished to pass new tax laws through parliament and at the same time conduct overdue budgetary negotiations with Hungary. By offering various concessions to the Czechs he thought to conclude a necessary truce with them and therefore, two months after he took office, ended

Top: The Czech social democrat František Soukup is giving a public speech (around 1910). In June 1912 Kafka attended a lecture by Soukup in the Municipal House.

17

Abendblatt.

Das Vaterland.

Zeitung für die österreichische Monarchie.

Telephon-Nummer der Redaction: 2543.   Telephon-Nummer des Expeditions- u. Inseraten-Bureaus: 2032.

Donnerstag, den 2. December 1897.   XXXVIII

Wien, 2. December.

Ueber Prag ist heute das Standrecht ver hängt worden. Zu dieser außerordentlich scharfen Maßregel ist in Oesterreich schon lange nicht mehr gegriffen worden. Die gestrigen Vorgänge in Prag lassen jedoch die Anwendung dieses Repressivmittels sowohl betreffend die Auffassung der jetzigen Lage als auch der bemnächst einzuschlagenden Taktik constatirt. Gegenüber der Behauptung der Presse der Obstructionisten kann hervorgehoben werden, daß die Position der beiden Parteien keineswegs durch den Regierungswechsel irgendwie erschüttert ist, sondern daß im Gegentheile sämmtliche Abgeordnete der erwähnten Parteien ruhig der weiteren Entwicklung entgegenleben fest entschlossen, die Ziele des gemeinschaftlichen Programmes nicht aus den Augen zu lassen und in entschei-

The Austrian newspaper "Fatherland" reports on the "December Storm" in Prague. Nationalistic riots had broken out and were only quelled by declaring martial law (1897).

Right: Mass assembly of the Czech national gymnastics organization "Sokol" on the Old Town Square (1912). 18,000 gymnasts demonstrated their gratitude to the "Slavic" host city Prague.

the civil state of emergency under which Prague had been governed for the past two years. With the new election reform act that he had passed through the Reichsrat (parliament) in June 1896, he hoped to subdue the "Young Czechs", whose party had grown to become the most significant power in the Czech camp and who had continually blocked the legislative process with their politics of obstruction. Soon Badeni was forced to realize that only a concession towards the Czech language demands could lead to success. Consequently, on April 5, 1897, he proclaimed language decrees for the Crown Lands of Bohemia (likewise, three weeks later, for Moravia) which provoked the most violent reactions, indeed, even a crisis of state.

According to the Badeni-decrees, promulgated without consulting the German representatives for Bohemia, the Czech and German languages were to be given equal status in the administrative structure of the crown lands of Bohemia. This would have forced a German civil servant in a German-Bohemian city like Reichenberg or Karlsbad to learn Czech if he wanted to follow a career in the civil service. In the German regions of Bohemia this initiative came as a real bombshell, especially given that the high numbers of Czech officials in the civil service had long been considered a provocation. In this battle of nationalities the Germans had expected support from Vienna, now they saw themselves betrayed by the Polish count, or worse still, humiliated. The waves of resentment were high; enough was enough. No accommodation was made for the fact that Czechs in Czech-speaking regions had had to accept German as the official language of administration for centuries. Most Czechs spoke German anyway, it was said, and besides, the circumstances were completely different.

In the face of these dangerous developments His Apostolic Majesty prorogued parliament on November 28, 1897. Count Badeni was dismissed. On the

The Austrian Emperor and (uncrowned) King of Bohemia Franz Joseph I (1903).

The morning edition of the *Prager Tablatt* reports on the foundation of the Czechoslovakian state as a sovereign Republic.

German side tempers cooled, but in December of the same year it was the Czechs' turn to vent their anger in wild riots on the streets of Prague combining anti-German feeling with anti-Semitism in what was later to become known as the "December Storm". Coffee houses, apartment houses, stores and flats were plundered; the badly injured and even the dead lay in the streets. It took army units with live ammunition to put an end to the anarchy, and martial law was declared. What remained was implacable hatred.

The central government in Vienna desperately tried to keep the situation under control by issuing emergency decrees, and the House of Hapsburg, indifferent in matters of nationality, stood as if paralyzed in front of the chasms that opened up between the people it ruled. Until the end, the Hapsburg dynasty tried to build bridges, but the luster of the monarchy of many peoples waned before the radiance of unified nation states. While the Czechs castigated tired old Austria as a prison for enslaved peoples, painting it in the darkest of colors, the sympathies of a growing number of Germans in Bohemia went out to the young and strong German

Nr. 251.   43. Jahrgang.   Morgen-Ausgabe.   Dienstag, 29. Oktober 1918

Die Errichtung des tschechoslowakischen Staates.

Völkerfreiheit!
Prag, 28. Oktober 1918.
Die zerbrochenen Wappenschilder des alten Oesterreich werden heute noch die Straßen Prags getragen. Eine neue Zeit erhebt sich aus den Scherben des alten, im Blut und Kot des vierjährigen Krieges erstickte. Wir alle müssen...

Das erste Gesetz des Nationalrates.
(C. B. B.) Prag, 28. Oktober. Das tschechoslowakische Preßbureau meldet:

Gesetz
erlassen vom Nationalausschuß am 28. Oktober 1918.

Die Uebergabe der Militärgewalt an den Nationalrat.
(C. B. B.) Prag, 28. Oktober. Das čechoslovakische Preßbureau teilt mit:
Als Vertreter des Militärkommandos in Böhmen erschienen um 9 Uhr abends JWK. Nestranek und JWK.

Reich. Particularly after the Badeni-crisis, they found in it a foil for the crumbling Austrian imperial state. In the Czech capital there was much talk of freedom and self-determination, of democratic renewal, re-building the empire, and finally also of renewal of a Czech sovereignty – certainly great words and noble goals. Then came the World War: in the *Material-schlachten* (battles in which superior numbers and re-sources – both men and equipment – are decisive), in the assaults of war, the last strength of once-mighty Austria gave out, and as it lay prostrate and defeated, the opportunity of a lifetime arose. The Czechs knew how to take advantage of it.

Thus, on October 28, 1918, a new era began. The young Czechoslovakia followed on the heels of a moribund Austria. The very name of this new state left no doubt who would have the most say in run-ning it. Millions of Czechs cheered and the voices of the few citizens of Prague who now looked to the future with trepidation could not make themselves heard above the frenzy of joy. These included Prague Germans who lost their jobs overnight, such as Kafka's superiors in the Workers' Accident Insurance Company, or the Prague Jews, loyal to their imperial pro-tectors to the last, who now feared the enmity of the Czech nationalists. Like-wise, Czech families loyal to the emperor may ultimately have comprised only a small minority; overnight, however, they found themselves on the wrong side. The place of the old, stooped emperor and his unhappy successor was occupied by the self-assured Tomáš G. Masaryk, a surro-gate emperor on horseback with his riding boots and crop. From one day to the next Kafka's old Prague had been transformed into the capital of a Slavic state immersed in a sea of blue, white and red flags.

The first Czechoslovakian president Tomáš Garrigue Masaryk (1931).

THE BEGINNINGS OF
THE KAFKA FAMILY IN PRAGUE

When a little son was born to the Jewish
fancy goods merchant Hermann Kafka
one year after his marriage, he must have
felt great joy – after all, this was a son
and heir who promised one day to follow in his father's footsteps. True, Hermann still stood at the beginning of his
career, yet the course had been set. He
had left the Bohemian hinterland, the
Czech village of Wossek in southern Bohemia, where he, the son of a Jewish
butcher, had been born in a poor hovel
in 1852 and where he had spent his childhood, to
come to Prague, the celebrated city on the Moldau.
In the capital such an enterprising young lad as he,
who had already done his compulsory military service and had no fear of hard work, could certainly get
somewhere. So Hermann opened a well located store
for haberdashery and fashion goods on the north side
of the Old Town Square.

Hermann Kafka (around
1885).

Hermann Kafka's parents presumably spoke German, but early on the young boy must also have
learned Czech. This was a matter of course for a shop-
keeper in multilingual Bohemia and was also a great
advantage in Prague. From an early age, Hermann
Kafka had had to lend a hand and work along with
his elders. He was therefore used to hard work. Because of this he never forgot the hardships of his
youth, when every morning at the break of dawn, be
it hot or cold, he had to leave home pulling a little
cart to visit his father's customers who were scattered
throughout the countryside. Hunger had also been a
frequent guest in the small thatched hovel.

In comparison, Kafka's mother Julie may have had
it easier in her youth. Her father was a former brew-
ery owner from Podiebrady, a small city on the upper

Hermann Kafka's fancy
goods store in the Kinsky
Palace, probably with original fixtures and fittings
(1946).

VELKOZÁVOD GALANTERNÍM, KRÁTKÝM
A STÁVKOVÝM ZBOŽÍM

Tovární sklad
pravých moravských
= PAPUČÍ =
švýc. vyšívání,
— krajek, —
trikového zboží
a
pánského prádla.

5eřman Kafka,

Praha I.,
Celetná ulice 3.

R. Schmelles, Praha

Hermann Kafka's business card (before 1906).

Franz Kafka in infancy (around 1884).

course of the Elbe River. He was not exactly rich, but the family earned a good living and wanted for nothing. When Julie's father was able to sell his property for a profit, he moved his whole family to Prague. When his daughter reached marriageable age she was entrusted to a "Schadchen", that is, to a Jewish marriage broker, who must have pulled Hermann Kafka's name out of a hat when suggesting him as a husband. Admittedly, Julie had also had to run her father's household and care for two younger brothers left behind after her mother's untimely death, so it wasn't difficult for her to stand by the husband who had been selected for her and tackle the work that had to be done in the store. The little Franz, to whom she gave birth on July 3, 1883, was meanwhile looked after by a nursery maid or wet-nurse, since Julie Kafka most likely did not have time to breastfeed him. His parents were battling laboriously, but ultimately successfully, through the difficult early years of a commercial venture. Although there was no lack of hired help, there was no question of a picturesque family idyll. His parents probably saw their little son only at mealtimes and in the evening, when they were too tired to play with him or to read or tell him stories. There was only time to play "Fran-cefus", a simple card game, which Mr and Mrs Kafka played when they sat down to rest after they had done their daily work.

Besides the tasks related to the store, the Kafkas had their hands full looking for a suitable apartment for their grow-ing family. In May 1885, when Franz was not even two years old, they moved their living quarters to 56 Wenceslas Square (II-802); a young Catholic maid by the name of Franziska Haas probably helped Frau Kafka with this. By Decem-ber of the same year we see the Kafkas once again packing their belongings and transporting them to a new home. They lived at 27 Geistgasse (Spirit Lane) (V-187) for only a few months. In the summer of 1887 it was on to the next abode: No 14 Niklas-straße (I-936); the following year they moved again, a few hundred meters to 2 Zeltnergasse (I-553). In July 1889, the family took up residence between the Old Town Square and the Kleiner Ring (Small Square) (I-3), in the immediate vicinity of the Old Town Hall, and settled down in a spacious apartment for at least three years.

Julie Kafka (around 1886).

Even if the young family didn't have many house-hold goods to transport from one place to another, all this moving around certainly represent a great drudgery involving formalities, worries, and all kinds of tasks. In addition to all that, Franz's mother was pregnant twice during these years and gave birth to two sons along the way. Their lives were short, how-ever: the first brother, Georg, born September 11, 1885, died of the then dreaded disease of measles on December 15, 1886, and Heinrich, the second brother, born on September 27, 1887, died in early in-fancy from meningitis. A robust nature was needed to be able to survive these blows of fate and to con-tinue to dedicate oneself resolutely to building up

25

First lines of Kafka's *Letter to Father* from 1919. "Dearest Father, You once asked me recently why I claim to be afraid of you. I did not know, as usual, what to answer, partly out of my fear of you and partly because the cause of this fear consists of too many details for me to put even halfway into words …"

and expanding the fancy goods store. In addition, there was trouble with the authorities after an anonymous denunciation: Hermann Kafka was accused of offering goods for sale on wooden shelves specially constructed for that purpose "on Sunday morning, when the crowd on the street is the greatest". The nails in the boards were said to present a danger to passers-by. Another time the charge was that Hermann Kafka had bought stolen goods. Although he managed to pull his head out of the noose each time, attacks like these must nonetheless have threatened to wear the family down. Worries and work from dawn till dusk. The parents didn't have much time for their son Franz in these years, since they were "always in the store", as he wrote later to his fiancée Felice Bauer. He, on the other hand, had to contend with "nurses, old nursemaids, malicious female cooks, sad governesses".

KAFKA'S PRAGUE ITINERARY

THE OLD TOWN SQUARE (ALTSTÄDTER RING)
Staroměstské náměstí

The best approach to the most important sites and stations of Kafka's life in Prague is by way of the Old Town Square (Altstädter Ring) in Prague's Old Town ("Altstadt"): the center of the city is at the same time the center of the author's world. The Kafka-sites that are clustered together in its immediate vicinity are the house in which he was born; the "Sixt House", in which the young Kafka family lived with the little boy for a period of a few months; the apartment-house "Of the Minute" ("Zur Minute"); as well as the Kinsky Palace, which housed Kafka's high school and also, for a number of years, his father's store. Julie Kafka lived in the Smetana-House at 20 Old Town Square (I-548) with her father and her half-brother

View of the Old Town Square and Tein Church (colorized postcard around 1910).

27

Old Town Square with the Old Town Hall and the House "Of the Minute" (four-color autotype, 1914).

Siegfried from July 1881 before becoming Hermann Kafka's wife. Right next door, in the house "Of Lazarus", 19 Old Town Square (I-549), the author's great uncle Leopold Kafka ran a coffee house. Directly beside the Sixt-House, number 16 (I-552), which once housed the bookshop "A. Štorch a syn", was the law office of Dr Richard Löwy, where, from April 1, 1906, Kafka gained his first professional experience articling as a law clerk. The so-called "Krenn-House" in front of St Nicholas' Church, formerly at 14 Niklasstraße (I-936), where Hermann Kafka's family lived from July 1887 until August 1888 no longer exists.

The Old Town Hall with the Apostles' Clock, which at that time still had its Neo-Gothic north wing; the beautiful townhouses on the south side of the square; the Gothic Tein Church with arcaded houses in front of it; the ponderously imposing St Nicholas' Church right next to Kafka's place of birth; the Kinsky Palace that juts so self-assuredly into the square; added to that the monumental statue of Jan Hus, erected during the First World War as a demonstration of Czech self-confidence; and the towering Baroque St Mary's Column, which marked the natural focal point of the square and provided the spot where the annual celebrations of the Virgin Mary took place on Assumption Day (August 15), that is, until it was torn down in 1918 as a symbol of Hapsburg rule – all this belonged to Kafka's familiar surroundings, was portrayed in his work, and formed an intimate part of his thoughts, imaginings, and dreams. The Old Town Square had provided the stage for the political and societal happenings that took place in the shadow of the castle on high, the Hradschin. It was the historic backdrop for events now so far removed as to seem legendary. There people were burned at the stake in the name of the inquisition and the bodies of executed city councilors and mayors had lain in their own blood. Revolutionaries, conspirators and common murderers had received their punishment there at the pillory, on the gallows, and on the wheel. The square had witnessed religious crusaders and Hussite mobs as well as furious Prague citizens fighting against the marauding mercenaries from the southern German city of Passau and the confused to-ing and fro-ing that followed the flight of the Winter King, Frederick of the Palatinate. On June 21, 1621, the rebellious Bohemian nobles had been paraded in front of the Old Town Hall and handed over to the headsman for execution. Again and again the clash of weapons of warring factions was heard here, the clang of lances, swords and knives, and more recently the thunder of cannon and the crack of rifles. Often enough alarm bells and drums had sounded a warning of invaders from Brandenburg, Sweden, Saxony, and France, Bavaria, and Prussia.

This was my high school here, in that building peeking through over there my university, and a little bit further on to the left my office. In this small circle … my whole life is encompassed.

Franz Kafka
to his Hebrew teacher
Friedrich Thieberger

View of the Old Town Hall with the then still existing north wing. The adjoining building to the right, the "Krenn-House", was pulled down around 1902 (colorized postcard, around 1902).

29

Old Town Square with Tein Church and the Tein School in front of it. Adjoining to the left is the House "Of the Stone Bell", then still with its Baroque decor, as well es the Kinsky Palace. To the right is the Baroque St Mary's Column.

But the annals of the Old Town Square also record more pleasant days: citizens were often enticed out of their houses by festive tournaments and pageantry, royal heads of state had ceremoniously entered the city, accompanied by shouts of jubilation and the ringing of bells, the roll of drums, and gun salutes. George of Podiebrady's election to the throne of Bohemia in 1458 met with the boundless enthusiasm of the inhabitants of Prague. These historic festive occasions were joined by folk festivals, parades, and concerts of military bands, as well as the celebrations determined by the Christian calendar: such as the annual Nikolai-Market at Christmas time, with its little stalls and attractions, or the Feast of Corpus Christi, when the churches, houses, and the square itself were decorated with flowers, wreaths or maypoles, and solemn processions passed by to the sounds of joyous song.

The House of Kafka's Birth, Formerly No 9 Niklasgasse

náměstí Franze Kafky 3 (I-24), Staré Město

The house in which Franz Kafka was born, a simple, two story house with flats on the northeast side of the Old Town Square, stood at the edge of the then still existing Prague ghetto. Although the location was central, towards the end of the 19th century the living conditions in the house on the corner of the Maiselgasse (Maisel Lane) and the Karpfengasse (Carp Lane) were rather on the modest side. The house had seen better times. It was built in the first half of the 18th century according to plans by the Czech architect František Maximilián Kaňka. Erected on the stone foundations of Romanesque buildings that had preceded

The memorial plaque on the wall of Kafka's birthplace.

The house in which Franz Kafka was born, the former prefecture of St Nicholas (around 1898).

Franz Kafka at the age of five (around 1888).

it, it was meant to serve as a private precinct for the prelates of the Slavic Benedictine monks, who had their abbey church in the neighboring St Nicholas' Church. The house, belonging to the monastery, was separated from the adjacent Jewish Quarter by a wall. The monks were not to use the building for long: When Emperor Joseph II ordered the dissolution of the monastery in 1785 the structure was bought by the city of Prague and used at first as an archive and storage place. From 1816 it served as a theater, and was finally used for residential purposes. Where once Benedictine monks had meditated, Jews moved in and the Christian building and the Niklasplatz (Nicholas' Square) in front of it gradually became a sort of antechamber to the Jewish Quarter.

Here on July 3, 1883, Franz Kafka was born, the first of six children of the newly married Hermann and Julie Kafka. As usual for homebirths, a midwife, Sofie Popper, was present. A few days after his birth, on July 10, the baby boy was circumcised by a Dr Moritz Weisl according to Jewish ritual. As his godfather the parents had chosen Angelus Kafka, his father's wealthy cousin. When in May 1885 the parents moved on to 56 Wenceslas Square (II-802) (a house which no longer exists), little Franz was not even two years old, much too young to have any memory of the place he was born.

In 1897 the house, which had been damaged in a fire, was torn down; a Neo-Baroque structure took its place. All that remained of the original house in which Kafka was born was the main portal with its balcony parapet, which was integrated into the new edifice. Since 1965 a bronze memorial bust has been mounted on one of the outside walls, fashioned by the Czech sculptor Karel Hladík after the communist leadership lifted its ban on Kafka in anticipation of the "Prague Spring".

A small exhibition and a shop on the ground floor of the house remind visitors of the famous writer who spent the first years of his life here.

THE SIXT-HOUSE IN THE ZELTNERGASSE
Celetná 2 (I-553), Staré Město

The narrow Zeltnergasse got its name from the "Czaltners", bakers of gingerbread, who at the beginning of the 14th century offered their wares for sale here. During Kafka's time it was an elegant shopping street, in which one could fulfill all one's needs. All the necessary tradespeople could be found there along with coffee houses and taverns, delicatessens, stores for hams and smoked meat, as well as confectionary shops, bookshops, dealers in art, paper or fashion, and stores for notions and fancy goods.

Between August 1888 and May 1889, the Kafka family lived in the Sixt-House, at the Old Town Square end of the lane. Its name comes from Sixt von Ottersdorf, who traded another building for this one in 1560 and whose family owned it until 1621. The history of the building, of course, reaches back much further: the still extant arch cross and barrel vault-construction from around 1220 indicates origins in the Romanesque period. Having stood here for more than 800 years, the building has experienced numerous expansions and reconstructions, and many illustrious personages are said to have lived here: the Roman tribune Cola di Rienzo for example, or Francesco Petrarch – even Dr Johannes Faust has been mentioned. The name of the Bohemian martyr Ludmilla, the grandmother of St Wenceslas, has also been connected with this house.

After the revolt of the nobles in 1621, the building was confiscated and put up for sale. It was then bought for 5,000 guilders by Philipp Fabricius Platter von Rosenfeld, the clerk of the Bohemian Chancellery who, in 1618,

View from the Powder Tower down Zeltnergasse (colorized postcard, around 1910).

was thrown out of a window in Prague Castle (Hradschin) in what became known as the "Defenestration of Prague". After a succession of owners the building passed to Wenzel and Anna Löschner in 1850. They still owned the Sixt-House at the time when Hermann Kafka and his young family rented a flat here for a brief period.

THE HOUSE "OF THE MINUTE" ("ZUR MINUTE") ON THE OLD TOWN SQUARE
Staroměstské náměstí 2 (I-3), Staré Město

After several years of wandering from one temporary domicile to another, the Kafka family moved into an apartment in the immediate vicinity of the Old Town Hall in July 1889. Their new home was located on the

Entrance to the tobacconist ("trafik") in the house "Of the Minute" (before 1910).

first floor of the house "Of the Minute" ("Zur Minute"), a late Gothic gabled house that had been rebuilt many times in the course of the 16th and 17th centuries. A lion gripping a shield with a coat of arms in its paws still acts as a reminder of the apothecary shop in which ointments were prepared and little potions brewed for almost 130 years until it closed its doors to the public forever in 1850. Before the turn of the century, when the Kafkas lived here, it housed a "trafik", that is, a shop selling tobacco, newspapers and similar articles "by the piece", or, as they say in Italy, "al minuto".

The Kafkas are thought to have remained at this address for three years, and little Franz spent a good deal of his primary schooldays here. The early childhood memories which he later related to his mistress Milena are reminiscences of the years in the house "Of the Minute", such as the story of the beggar woman on the Kleiner Ring (Small Square): "Once, as a very small boy, I was given a sixpence and felt a great urge to give it away to an old woman who was begging at a spot right between the Big Square [Old Town Square] and the Small Square. This sum of money, however, really seemed to me to be enormous, such a huge sum as had never been given to a beggar before. Therefore I was ashamed to carry out such an extravagant gesture in her presence. But give it to her I must, so I had it broken down into small change, gave the beggar woman a ha'penny, ran around the whole block of the Town Hall and the arcades on the Small Square and returned to her from the left side of the square as a completely new benefactor, again gave the woman a ha'penny, started off on my run again and did that happily ten times (or somewhat less, since I think the

One of Kafka's adresses: The house "Of the Minute" with Renaissance sgraffitos (after 1900).

The Renaissance sgraffiti, dating from before 1615, depicting themes from the Bible and ancient myths, were painted over at Kafka's time. The arcade was also still closed off to the public at the turn of the century and was only opened in 1938.

35

beggar woman lost patience at one point and disappeared from under my nose). In any case, in the end I was so exhausted, morally too, that I ran straight home and cried for such a long time that my mother replaced my sixpence."

When Hermann and Julie Kafka were expecting yet another child, after a son and two daughters (Elli and Valli), they soon began to look out for bigger living quarters. The Kafka family business was now profitable enough for them to afford a comfortable home. Thus, we see the family descending the stairs of the house "Of the Minute" with bag and baggage in 1892 and heaving their accumulated household goods onto the cart that was to move them to a new home. Kafka's sisters toddled behind it, maybe with dolls in their arms, but Franz probably helped to the best of his ability.

THE K. K. (IMPERIAL, ROYAL) STATE GERMAN-LANGUAGE PRIMARY SCHOOL FOR BOYS IN PRAGUE – OLD TOWN
Masná 18 (I-1000), Staré Město

On September 16, 1889, a Monday in early fall, the young Franz, a slim little boy, started out on his way to the German Primary School for Boys in the Fleisch-marktgasse (Meat Market Street) for the first time. Hans Markert, his classroom teacher, directed him and other children of his age to their seats on the wooden school benches. After a few measured words, spoken beneath the picture of his Imperial Majesty Franz Joseph, the boys were then immediately dismissed and returned to the care of their waiting mothers. Just a short ceremony and yet it marked an important new beginning – for Franz Kafka, life's serious side had begun, but so had a time of new horizons beyond the narrow confines of the parental house, a time for laughter, "which in its innocent sincerity is only given to primary students on their school benches." Admittedly it was also a time of fear, since Kafka always despaired of living up to the academic standards of the school: "Never would I get through first grade, I thought, but it happened and I even got a prize."

Kafka's path to school led from the house "Of the Minute", where the family lived, past the complex of buildings which formed the Town Hall with its famous Astronomical Clock directly

Top left: Kafka as an elementary school student with his sisters Elli (right) and Valli around 1890.

Bottom left: The "Small Square" with its medieval arcades (around 1907).

Bottom: Excerpt from Franz Kafka's secondary school leaving certificate.

37

The Classicistic school building, dating from the years before 1853, rebuilt in a Neo-Renaissance style between 1874 and 1879, is used as an apartment building today.

A school class in Prague around the turn of the century. On the far left, in the first row, is the Prague-German poet Johannes Urzidil.

across the Old Town Square, past the St Mary's Column, toward the Tein Church. Between the church and the then still Baroque exterior of the house "Of the Stone Bell" ("Zur Steinernen Glocke") ran the narrow little passage, the Teingasse, which led either across the Tein Courtyard or past the side of the Tein Courtyard into the Fleischmarktgasse.

In the immediate vicinity of the German Primary School, as Hugo Bergmann described it in his memoir *Schooldays and Studies* (*Schulzeit und Studium*), there stood a Czech school which competed with the German one, with a bust of the Czech pedagogue Jan Ámos Komenský prominently displayed at its entrance, the words written beneath it revealing a political agenda: "A Czech child belongs in a Czech school!" Those were years when the German School Association and its Czech counterpart, the Matice česká, struggled bitterly for each and every school child.

The k. u. k. (Imperial and Royal) State German-Language Secondary School (High School) in Prague – Old Town
Staroměstské náměstí 12 (I-606 and I-607), Staré Město

The 10th September 1893 was a memorable day for the now ten-year-old Franz – his first school day in the first level of the State German Language High School in the Old Town of Prague. Enrollment in this humanistic high school was subject to an entrance exam in religion, German, and mathematics, which Kafka passed without much trouble. Now four years of lower high school (the four levels being Prima, Sekunda, Tertia, Quarta) in the Kinsky Palace lay ahead of Kafka and, if he passed those with sufficiently good grades, four further years on a higher level leading to the crowning achievement of earning the leaving certificate (the Matura), at that time a monstrous exam anticipated with extreme trepidation. The individual school year stretched over ten months from September to June, with a few days off scheduled in February. Class trips and other such departures from the regular lessons were rare. From an early stage, pupils were asked to show comportment and willingness to achieve; whoever did not measure up to the demands had to leave. After their daily studies, homework, reading schedules, tutoring, and preparations for exams, pupils had very little time for other interests, let alone for useless games and leisure time.

The Kinsky Palace, one of the most beautiful noble palaces in Prague, is a mature and late work of the architect Kilian Ignaz Dientzenhofer, executed

Bottom: Franz Kafka at about the age of ten (around 1893).

With the exception of mathematics, for which he did not have the greatest aptitude and liking, Kafka showed good ability in all subjects, according to the annual school reports of the first three years, he even achieved distinction.

The Kinsky Palace on the Old Town Square (around 1910).

between 1755 and 1765 by the Italian master builder Anselmo Lurago. The decorative work on the outside of the building comes from the workshop of Ignaz Franz Platzer while the Empire style entrance and stairway within the building date from the 1830s. The town palace was originally built for Johann Arnold von Goltz and did not come into the possession of the Kinsky family until 1786. Bertha von Suttner, born in 1843 as Bertha Sophia Felicita, Countess Kinsky of Chinic and Tettau, the well-known pacifist author and first Nobel Peace Prize Winner, spent the early years of her childhood here. In 1871 the high school in which Kafka passed his first four years, was established in the building's courtyard-wing, erected in the years 1836 to 1839. The last four years of high school Kafka spent in classrooms located on the second floor of the front wing. After 1911 the institution continued as the first Prague German Modern (i. e. scientifically oriented) High School. In 1924 it closed its doors forever.

From October 1912 to June 1918 the town palace with its unique Rococo façade also housed the retail

Franz Kafka after graduating from secondary school (1901).

store of Hermann Kafka – a truly select address. After the Second World War the rightful owners of the palace, the noble Kinsky family, were expropriated by the infamous presidential decrees of Edvard Beneš. On February 21, 1948, the Stalinist Prime Minister Klement Gottwald proclaimed the resignation of the bourgeois ministers from the balcony of the palace, and, by doing so, completed the communist takeover of power in Czechoslovakia.

Today, one of the collections of the National Gallery is located in this elegant structure jutting out into the square on a wide front, while demands for restitution to its rightful owners have attracted significant media attention recently. Since 1995, a bookshop on the premises of the former store has reminded the visitor of the Kafka family business.

THE HOUSE "OF THE THREE KINGS" ("ZU DEN DREI KÖNIGEN") IN THE ZELTNERGASSE
Celetná 3 (I-602), Staré Město

The new abode the Kafkas moved into in 1892 was located in the two-story house "Of the Three Kings", a building from the late Gothic period in the Zeltnergasse, mentioned in records dating back as far as 1365. In the 18th century the façade was done over in the Baroque manner and the house assumed its present look. The "Pawlatschen" (roofed-in, arcade-like balconies on each floor) looking out onto the inside courtyard were added in 1860. The second story apartment with narrow, angular and ancient, but friendly rooms facing right out onto the Tein Church had one undeniable advantage for Franz Kafka: his own room, to the left of the dining room, simply furnished with a bed and wash basin, night table, bookcase, and wardrobe. "The door was constantly open", the governess Anna Pouzarová related decades later. To have one's own room was in no way a matter of course for a Prague high school boy, as Kafka's friend and classmate Hugo Bergmann confirms: "We both were friends from earliest boyhood on. Franz's mother knew my mother and so I soon became a companion of Franz in their house in the Zeltnergasse. The fact that even as a young school boy Franz had his own room and that from its window one could look down on the Zeltnergasse, yes, that he even had his own desk made a great impression on me."

In the house "Of the Three Kings" Kafka took his first steps in literature, though he destroyed

Left: The maze of roofs, chimneys, and "Pawlatschen" (covered courtyard verandas) in the Old Town.

Bottom: Pen drawing by Franz Kafka from a series that Max Brod later named "Black Marionettes on Invisible Strings".

most of these early works from his school and student days. In this young man who stands at the window we are yet to see the unsurpassed writer, rather a shy, thin, tall, spindly student in his fourth year of high school.

The paternal store had already been transferred into the house "Of the Three Kings" in 1887, so that now family home and firm were under one roof. The father's business continued to thrive. Its circle of customers expanded and, in the meantime, he himself had even advanced to become an officially appointed and sworn-in expert at the k.u.k. (Imperial and Royal) Commercial Court. Hermann Kafka worked day and night; his wife Julie proved to be a dependable helper and support in his endeavors. After a retail business came wholesale – the Kafkas knew that one had to strike while the iron was hot. Their son, of course, was less interested in that aspect, although his parents still continued to think that he would some day take over the business. Entry into a career was in the distant future, school and university opened new horizons that went far beyond the commercial goals of his father.

By as early as around 1906 Hermann Kafka could apparently afford to give up the laborious retail shop and moved what had now become an exclusively wholesale business for "fancy goods, notions, knit-wear", as well as for "genuine Moravian 'Papuči' (Slippers), Swiss embroidery, lace, tricots, and men's underwear" a few houses further down the street to 12 Zeltnergasse (I-558). About a year later, in May 1907, the Kafkas also said farewell to the apartment at No 3 Zeltnergasse. They had lived there for fifteen years during which time the little boy had grown into a student of 24 years of age. Kafka probably looked out of the window distractedly onto the narrow street for one last time before his personal belongings were carefully bundled together and carried downstairs, for, naturally, old houses like that had no elevators. His bicycle, on the other hand, might not have been loaded onto the horse-drawn wagon used for the move. It was just a short ride to the Kafka family's new abode.

Left: The entrance to the house at No 12 Zeltnergasse with the sign for Hermann Kafka's fancy goods whole-sale business (around 1906).

Among his possessions the young man counted an old, small, almost black desk placed right next to the door at which he could study and do his homework. Over the desk hung a large repro-duction of a painting, to the side on the wall a plaster of paris copy of a Roman relief. One day, his high school diploma lay on the desk, attesting to his academic maturity and marking the end of his time in secondary school. Soon the volumes he needed for his univer-sity studies – in Roman law, common law, com-mercial, civil, and crim-inal law, to name just the most important sub-jects – were piled high on the same desk. He spent many years of his youth bent over his books in the Zeltnergasse, and even while the young articling clerk was put-ting the obligatory year of practical law training at court behind him, he still lived in the room he first had as a child.

45

THE CHARLES BRIDGE (KARLSBRÜCKE)
Karlův most

From as early as the 14th century onwards, the Gothic Charles Bridge spanned the Moldau, probably the most beautiful monument to the building prowess of the Middle Ages. When its 12th century predecessor, the stone Judith Bridge, fell victim to massive ice floes in the Moldau in 1342, a new bridge had to be erected across its waters. First of all, the court astrologer was commissioned to divine the most propitious date to begin building: In the year 1357, on the 9th day of the 7th month, at 5.31 a.m., Emperor Charles the

Fourth was to lay the cornerstone to the new bridge. The young master builder Peter Parler from Schwäbisch Gmünd (in southern Germany), to whom the work had been entrusted, did not lose any time in beginning, nonetheless construction dragged on into the 16th century. But in the end there was something to show for it: the bridge's sixteen arches span the Moldau River and for a good half a millenium remained the only connection between the Old Town and the Lesser Town (Kleinseite). Although folklore tells a number of legends extolling its strength, the Charles Bridge did nonetheless once fall down. On September 4, 1890, the sixth and seventh arches could no longer withstand the pressure of the flood waters – statues toppled into the deep and two people drowned. For two whole years the principal connection between the Old Town and the Lesser Town remained closed to general traffic!

Many a historic event also took place on the Charles Bridge; in the Thirty Years' War, for example, the citizens of Prague beat back the Swedes who were advancing on the Old Town in a heroic fight. A good part of the façades on the Old Town Bridge Tower were destroyed in the attack, but just before they got to the crucifix on the bridge, the mercenaries from the north were forced to sound their retreat.

The first of the bridge's total of thirty statues was put in place in 1657: the cast iron crucifix to which a Hebrew inscription was added in 1696. The second statue was the bronze figure of St Nepomuk cast in Nuremberg in 1683. From here, a whole Nepumuk-cult extended over all of Europe: since that time innumerable statues of the saint have guarded bridges and crossings, proclaiming his martyrdom on the Charles Bridge.

In a simple three-verse poem he wrote in 1903 for his friend Oskar Pollak, a young Kafka paid homage to the bridge and its saints:

Left: The Old Town end of the stone Charles Bridge with the Crusaders' Monastery and towers of the Old Town. At the far left, the cupola of St Nicholas' Church next to the house of Kafka's birth (around 1870).

Below: A maid crossing Charles Bridge, in the background the Gothic Lesser Town Bridge Tower (around 1910).

47

Below: The partly collapsed Charles Bridge with flotsam and debris after the floods of 1890.

Top right: The official seal of Prague's Charles University.

Bottom right: The "Stone Student of Prague" in one of the courtyards of the Clementinum. The statue commemorates the defense of Prague against the Swedes by students in 1648. It became an important symbol for the proud tradition of German students in Prague.

"People who walk over dark bridges,
   Past holy stone saints
   With feeble light upon them.

Clouds that wander over gray skies
   Past churches
   With fading towers.

Someone who leans on the stone parapet
   And looks into the evening water
   His hands resting on old stones."

When Kafka ambled across the Charles Bridge to the Lesser Town, which must have happened often, he could marvel at the stone witnesses to Catholic religiosity which was still alive and vibrant in Prague.

THE PRAGUE UNIVERSITY
Železná 9 / Ovocný trh 3 (I-541), Staré Město

The University of Prague was founded by Emperor Charles the Fourth of Luxembourg on April 7, 1348, as the first university north of the Alps. All that remains from the early days of this significant seat of higher learning are the Gothic alcove balcony of the Chapel of SS Cosmas and Damian, built in 1370, a vaulted hallway and the great university hall, which is still used today for academic ceremonies.

The history of the university throughout the centuries mirrors the history of Bohemia: After initially flourishing at the beginning of the 15th century, it was forced into decline by the so-called "Decree of Kuttenberg" ("Kuttenberger Dekret") of 1409 in which King Wenceslas the Fourth yielded to the nationalistic demands of the rector Jan Hus. According to the decree the "natio Bohemica" (Bohemian nation), to which both German and Czech subjects in the crown lands belonged, was to have three votes in the self-governance of the university in contrast to the one vote for each of the other nations represented: Bavaria, Saxony, and Poland. Consequently, a great number of students, university teachers, and professors left the Charles College in order to take up their studies at other universities. University cities such as Kraków, Heidelberg, Vienna and Cologne blossomed; in Leipzig a new university even came into being. Until the university was taken over by the Jesuits in the year 1622 and merged with the Clementinum to form the Karl-Ferdinand University, it was reviled as a breeding ground for heretics.

In the 19th and 20th centuries, too, the university was the scene of political feuds. In the era of the most vehement national rivalry between Germans and Czechs it was decided to

split the university into a German and a Czech one. That did not put an end to the quarrel which persisted until the beginning of the Second World War. On November 17, 1939, the Czech university was closed on the orders of the German Reichsprotektor; upon his return home from his London exile in 1945 the Czechoslovakian president Edvard Beneš decreed the retroactive dissolution of the German university. On two more occasions the Charles University would play an important role in the political history of the country: during the days of the so-called "Prague Spring" of 1967 /68 and in 1989, when the student body played a key part in the "Velvet Revolution", fifty years to the day after the bureaucrats of the German Protectorate shut down the Czech university.

After receiving his high school leaving certificate and following a few weeks of vacation on the German North Sea islands of Norderney and Helgoland, Kafka took up his studies at the German Karl-Ferdinand University in Prague in the winter semester of 1901/02. For the first two weeks he tried studying chemistry, then in the end registered in the faculty of law. In the summer semester of 1903, Kafka attended lectures given by the eminent Prague Germanist Professor

August Sauer, but could not decide whether to switch over to German studies permanently. Kafka remained with the law faculty until he graduated and received his doctorate. Admittedly he did not want to become a practicing lawyer, but he thought he would surely find a position as a law clerk in the bureaucracy of the state, although he knew Jews were not exactly welcomed with open arms. There were possibilities for the future in banks, insurance companies, in the postal system, or in commerce and industry – the legal profession was a good way to earn one's daily bread.

After the summer vacation of 1905 the period of carefree student pleasures was over. The final exams loomed on the horizon and with them a period in which Kafka "with a copious sacrifice of nerves fed [his] intellect literally on sawdust which (…) in addition had been chewed by thousands of mouths before", as he remembered in his *Letter to Father (Brief an den Vater)*. Visits to coffee houses, literary and philosophical excursions, and undertakings among his

Student life in Prague:

Top left: A poster of the "Reading and Debating Society of the German Students in Prague", the umbrella organization of the liberal German students. Kafka joined the "Hall", as it was called, when he took up his studies. He was especially committed to the "Literature and Arts" section.

Bottom left: Members of a Prague student corps with their typical caps, known as "lids" (around 1900).

Top: Members of several student corps spike their caps in honor of the sovereign. The tradition of this solemn student ritual, called "Landesvaterstechen", has its roots in the 18th century (oil painting by Oscar Rex, around 1900).

51

The Fruit Market. The State Civil Court (see p. 55) is the dark buildung left of the center (postcard around 1900).

The lectures in law took place in the principal building of the university, the "Carolinum", which one entered at 9 Eisengasse (Iron Lane). Kafka also attended the law department at No 5 Obstmarkt (Fruit Market) (I-560) and the political science department that was housed in the Clam-Gallas Palace at No 20 Husgasse (I-158).

circle of friends had to be postponed to the time after graduation. Three oral exams still separated Kafka from the title of Doctor of Jurisprudence, three exams in which the sum of his knowledge of law was to be determined: first the Rigorosum II had to be passed, a test of his knowledge of civil, commercial, and exchange law. On November 7, 1905, Kafka mastered this hurdle, gaining three out of four examiners' votes. Riding high on a wave of self-confidence he now also registered for the Rigorosum III, for which general legal topics and Austrian constitutional law, international law, and political economy were on the list. And on March 16, 1906, he also passed this exam, although at the last minute Kafka had thought of excusing himself from the exam on the grounds of illness.

Now there remained only the Rigorosum I: Roman, canonical and German law. On June 13, 1906, Kafka cleared this last hurdle too and only five days later, on June 18, he was ready to be awarded the degree of Doctor of Laws in an age-old ceremony held in the convocation hall of the Karl-Ferdinand University in Prague.

The Café Louvre
In the Former Ferdinandstrasse
Národní třída 22 (II-116), Nové Město

The Café Louvre represents one of the last classically elegant coffee houses from the era of the old Austria. It was established in 1902 on the first floor of a former city palace on the Ferdinandstraße, the Czech corso, that is, the street in which the Czechs traditionally like to stroll. The public were welcomed into a mirrored foyer, and large rooms flooded with natural light and decorated with old prints on the walls. In addition, the coffee house offered bright billiard rooms (in which the Prague Billiard Club held its annual competitions) and spacious rooms for chess – there were even writing rooms equipped with telephones, while anyone wishing to be alone could retire to the "chambres particulières", the private drawing rooms. The exclusive clientele was treated to concerts in the café twice a day. The pretty profiles of many young Czech women

Bottom: The Café Louvre in Ferdinand Street (1907).

Next page: The main hall of the Café Louvre (1910).

Max read the first act of 'Farewell to Youth' (Abschied von der Jugend) to me. How can I in my present state today measure up to this; I'd have to search a whole year before I could find a genuine feeling in me and now, in a coffee house, late at night, plagued by the wayward flatulence of a – despite every effort – bad digestion, I'm supposed to be allowed with some incomprehensible justification to remain seated on my chair and listen to such a great work.

Diary entry by Kafka
on January 17, 1911

were reflected in the mirrors – women, who at the turn of the century had begun to exchange their tea parties at home for visits to a coffee house. Franz Kafka and Max Brod were not the only ones to spend "pleasant, peaceful hours" there, as Brod described them in his diary on November 7, 1907 – so did Felix Weltsch, Otto Pick, Franz Werfel, and František Langer, to name only a few.

Soon after the coffee house opened, a German philosophical circle met once every other week in one of the private conference rooms facing the inner courtyard to discuss the teachings of Franz Brentano, then a very popular philosopher in Prague, a former priest and professor at the University of Vienna. Its members included the Prague philosophers Oskar Kraus, Emil Utitz, as well as Max Brod, who in his autobiography counts these meetings among his life's most pleasant memories: "The nice thing about this circle was that it didn't possess the slightest trace of the usual club 'busybodyness', one had the feeling that pure truth and research were being served."

At first Kafka also went along but when Brod was kicked out in 1905 because of the "intrigues of one single person", Kafka also broke off his connection with the Brentano circle – without, of course, stopping his visits to the Café Louvre.

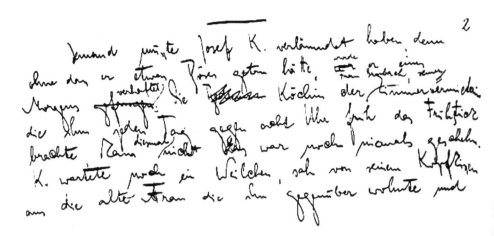

THE STATE CIVIL COURT ON THE OBSTMARKT (FRUIT MARKET)

Ovocný trh 14 / Celetná 36 (I-587), Staré Město

Top: The first lines of Kafka's manuscript for his novel *The Trial.*

Bottom: The State Civil Court.

On October 1, 1906, Kafka began the internship required of a law student, first at the State Civil Court at 14 Obstmarkt (Fruit Market), then at the State Criminal Court on the Karlsplatz (Charles Square), a Neo-Renaissance building erected between 1900 and 1903. Grudgingly, he subjected himself to the year of law practice and thought he would be compelled to "die like a dog". Max Brod, too, worked here as a young jurist. The endless halls and the countless courtrooms and waiting rooms are said to have served Kafka as models for his novel *The Trial (Der Prozeß)*.

The building, which dates back to a medieval town house opening onto the Zeltnergasse, served as a mint until the year 1783. From 1784 on the k. k. War Chancellery and the Prague general military command were located here. Then, from 1850 onwards, it was the seat of the State Civil Court. For this reason, the Neo-Baroque extension opening onto the Obstmarkt (Fruit Market) was completed in the years 1857–1861. The figures holding up the balcony, created by Ignaz Franz Platzer, show miners and soldiers.

55

The House "Of the Ship" ("Zum Schiff") in the Former Niklasstrasse

Pařížská 36 (I-883), Staré Město (no longer extant)

In June 1907 the Kafka family had moved from the medieval house "Of the Three Kings" into the more elegant Niklasstraße. The apartment building "Of the Ship" was one of the palatial apartment buildings that had grown up on the razed area of the old Prague ghetto. Although the house belonged to a Czech jeweler named Alfréd Nikodém, it was for the most part let to German tenants. During these years both Hermann Kafka and Nikodém had stores in the Zeltnergasse. Besides the middle-class merchants living on the mezzanine, the first, second and third floors, a student inhabited the mansard room, two sales girls, a tanner's assistant and his wife lived in the garret, and a custodian with his family on the ground floor. If one wanted to enter the locked house after ten at night, the latter had to be paid the "Sperrsechserl", the "locking-sixpence" (for unlocking and locking up again).

From the apartment on the third floor one looked down on the end of the Niklasstraße leading to the new Svatopluk Čech Bridge, where a toll-keeper fulfilled his duty. Furthermore, a unique panorama opened up beyond the Moldau: on the left-hand side appeared the Observation Tower on the Laurenziberg (Mount St Lawrence), then the church towers of the Premonstratensian monastery of Strahov, finally the steeple of St Vitus' Cathedral and the Prague Castle (Hradschin), as well as the Belvedere Palace and the green slopes of the Belvedere Heights with the Hanau Pavilion. Across the river, on which anglers drifted in their rowboats, Kafka could see the "Zivilschwimmschule" (the Civilian Swimming School), a public swimming establishment which he liked to visit in summer.

FRANZ KAFKA

DIE VERWANDLUNG

DER JÜNGSTE TAG · 22/23
KURT WOLFF VERLAG · LEIPZIG
1 9 1 6

Left: View of Niklasstraße and the Old Town from the Belvedere Heights (around 1910). In the foreground are the towers of the Čech Bridge, behind them the corner house "Of the Ship". The Kafkas' apartment was located on the top floor of the building. Franz Kafka's room was to the right of the room with the balcony.

Top: The jacket of the first edition of Franz Kafka's short story *The Metamorphosis* with a cover illustration by Ottomar Starke (1915).

The Metamorphosis (Die Verwandlung) was among the pieces conceived in this apartment, and the layout of its rooms is clearly reproduced in that work: Just as in the house "Of the Ship", Gregor Samsa lived in a lofty room with side doors leading to adjacent rooms, one on the left, one on the right, and a third door leading into an antechamber or vestibule. Kafka included various of these details in the story, for example: "The reflection of the electric street lights lay in pale pools here and there on the ceiling and on the upper parts of the furniture".

In the house "Of the Ship" on the night of September 22 to 23, 1912, Kafka wrote down the famous story *The Judgment (Das Urteil)*, "like a regular birth covered with filth and slime": "I wrote the story 'the Judgment' in one fell swoop during the night of the 22nd to the 23rd from ten o'clock at night until six in the morning. I could hardly move my legs from under the desk, so stiff had they grown from sitting so long. The terrible exertion and joy, the way the story developed before my eyes, the way I plowed through the waters. Numerous times during this night

The Secession style Svatopluk Čech Bridge (around 1910).

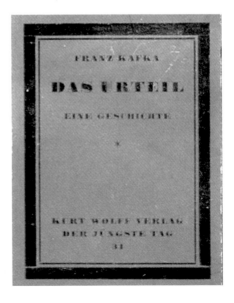

Top: Page from the manuscript of *The Judgment* (1912):

"It was a most beautiful Sunday morning in springtime. Georg Bendemann, a young merchant, sat in his own room on the second floor of one of those low, shoddily built houses that stretched along the river in a long row, differing from each other only slightly in height and color. He had just finished a letter to a childhood friend who lived abroad, sealed it with deliberate languidness …"

I carried the full burden of my weight on my back. The way everything can be risked, the way that for all ideas, even for the strangest flashes of inspiration, a great flame is prepared in which they perish and rise again. The way the blue dawn appeared at my window, a cart drove by, two men walked over the bridge. At 2 o'clock I looked at the clock for the last time. When the maid passed through the vestibule for the first time I wrote down the last sentence. Extinguishing the lamp and the light of day. The slight pains around the heart. Tiredness which disappeared in the middle of the night. My trembling entrance to my sisters' room. Reading to them. Before that stretching my body in front of the maid and saying: 'I've written up till now.' The appearance of the untouched bed as if it had been carried into the room this minute. The confirmed conviction that in my novel writing I find myself in the shameful depths of writing. Only in this way can one write, only with such continuity, with such complete opening of body and soul. Morning in bed."

In the last days of the war in 1945, the house "Of the Ship" was destroyed in an artillery barrage and the ruins then razed. A hotel building from the 1970s now rises up where the house once stood.

Bottom: Cover detail of the first edition of Franz Kafka's *The Judgment*. The short story was published as part of Kurt Wolff's *Judgment Day* series.

THE ASSICURAZIONI GENERALI ON WENCESLAS SQUARE
Václavské náměstí 19 (II-832), Nové Město

The first thing Kafka did after obtaining his doctorate in law was to take a vacation in the country at the house of his favorite uncle, Siegfried Löwy, in the Moravian town of Triesch. For the time being there were no job prospects, perhaps due partly to the fact that his exam marks had not been the best. Therefore, the family tried to make use of its connections. The financial manager of the Union Bank in Prague, Arnold Weissberger, was probably asked to put in a good word for the young man. Weissberger's son was the director of the Madrid branch office of the Assicurazioni Generali (one of the largest European insurance companies with head offices in Trieste) and could easily find a place for Kafka in the Prague branch. But perhaps the applicant also owed his job to Max Brod, for he was a good friend

of the director of the Prague Generali, Ernst Eisner, a well-educated and art-loving relative of Paul Eisner, the Prague-based writer and specialist in German studies.

On the first of October 1907 Kafka began work in the Generali, which had its prestigious Bohemian head office on Wenceslas Square in a Neo-Baroque city palace built in 1896. To Miss Hedwig Weiler, a young Jewish girl he had fallen in love with in Triesch, he wrote of his aspirations: "Now in the office. I am employed with the Assicurazioni Generali and have the hope despite everything of seeing myself seated in a comfortable office chair in distant lands some day, looking out onto sugar cane fields or Mohammedan graveyards from the office window, and insurance itself interests me a lot, but the work I'm doing at the moment is dreary. And yet it's sometimes quite nice to put down my pen and to imagine placing one of your hands on top of the other and enfolding them with one of my hands and to know now that I wouldn't let them go, not even if someone were to unscrew my hand at the wrist."

It took only a few weeks before Kafka started to look around for a new position. Although his literature-loving superior, director Ernst Eisner, treated him with benevolence, the time he spent at work in the Generali was, he felt, too long, and his dreams of distant lands with a view of "Mohammedan graveyards" and similar exotic things turned out to be imaginary daydreaming. Kafka worked as a supplemental assistant daily from eight in the morning frequently until eight-thirty at night with only seven days paid vacation per year and eighty crowns monthly salary. The activity in the office was brisk and demanded complete commitment of all one's energy.

Franz Kafka at the beginning of his professional career (around 1907).

Left: The building of the Assicurazioni Generali on Wenceslas Square built in 1896 (colorized postcard, around 1903).

THE HOUSE OF THE FORMER GERMAN BUSINESS ACADEMY
Masná 8 (I-620), Staré Město

The German Business Academy, a school held in high esteem by Prague business circles, was founded in 1856 and was the first commercial institute of higher learning within the confines of the Hapsburg monarchy. The so-called "Redoute", a hall for concerts and balls, had been located in the two story building in the Fleischmarktgasse (Meat Market Street) since the second half of the 18th century, where no less a figure than Carl Maria von Weber held concerts in 1813.

The Business Academy was considered part of the German establishment in Prague, resulting in its devastation in the "December Storm" of 1897: "Everywhere in the vicinity German and Jewish shops and living quarters were broken into and plundered. When enraged mobs also assembled in front of our house, the house 'Of the Black Lamb', and we heard the calls: 'Germans! Jews!', our maid, a Czech girl herself, had torn open the kitchen window and called out to the rioters: 'No Germans living here, but over there, that's the German Business Academy!' One hour later, furniture, equipment, and pictures from the German Business Academy lay on the streets in pieces – but nothing had been done to our house, not even the window panes had been broken."

From the 3rd of February to the 20th of May 1908, Kafka had attended an evening course of studies for high school students in the Academy on the topic of worker's insurance. The curriculum included "Development of Workers' Insurance in the European Coun-

A postcard of a Prague student corps showing the riots during the "December Storm" (around 1900).

Die Revolte in Prag.
Deutsche Studenten, welche einen verwundeten Collegen nach Hause führen wollen, werden vom Pöbel überfallen. 30. November 1897.

Gruß aus

tries and in Austria" taught by the university lecturer Dr Marschner, later to be Kafka's boss. From his later immediate superior at the Workers' Accident Insurance Company, Eugen Pfohl, Kafka learned about the "Comprehensive Agenda of Accident Insurance (mandatory insurance, classification of factories, premium payment scales, and control of premium income)" as well as statistics. The lectures by Kafka's later colleague Dr Fleischmann dealt with the "Special Law of Health Insurance" (mandatory insurance, organization and detailed management of the financing of health insurance). To top it all off Kafka received instruction in the "Basic Principles of Simple and Double-Entry Bookkeeping" as well as in "Bookkeeping in Health and Accident Insurance". Equipped with these specialized areas of knowledge, Kafka hoped to be able to lend some well-earned weight to his application for a position at the Prague Workers' Accident Insurance Company.

The building of the Prague German Business Academy (around 1900).

The schoolrooms were situated on the first and second floors of the Classicistic structure.

The Workers' Accident Insurance Company for the Kingdom of Bohemia
Na Poříčí 7 (II-1075), Nové Město

Kafka had his classmate Ewald Felix Příbram to thank for being admitted to the job of auxiliary official in the Workers' Accident Insurance Company for the Kingdom of Bohemia in Prague (Arbeiter-Unfall-Versicherungs-Anstalt für das Königreich Böhmen in Prag, or, short: AUVA) on July 30, 1908. Ewald's father, Dr Otto Příbram, had been president of the Company since 1895. He smoothed the way for the acceptance of the inexperienced graduate. Among the 250 employees there was besides Kafka only one Jew, Dr Siegmund Fleischmann, the Company Secretary. Thus it was quite natural that Kafka was assigned to him as an auxiliary official. A letter from his doctor enabled him to take leave swiftly and elegantly from his old post at the Generali.

Kafka's working day ran from eight in the morning until two in the afternoon in what was called a "single cycle" ("einfache Frequenz"); this meant no work in the afternoon, hardly longer than a half-time position. Moreover, in the AUVA he could look forward to a civil service pension and the remuneration was noticeably higher – all in all therefore it was a marked improvement over the conditions offered by the Generali. Despite Kafka's continual complaints about his hated duties at work, he developed into an experienced expert in insurance within a few years. At first he was charged with the classification of the companies that fell within his domain into danger categories, visiting them, and doing on-site inspections. After he had become acquainted with this work, Kafka was entrusted with representing the Company in court, asked to produce statistics, to independently conduct correspondence on behalf of the Company, and to attend to accident prevention and job safety which was still in its infancy. During the war years the range of his tasks changed, since the war casualties –

Left: The residence of the Workers' Accident Insurance Company. Kafka's office was at first on the top floor, later on the first floor.

Top: The bilingual seal of the Workers' Accident Insurance Company for the Kingdom of Bohemia in Prague (before 1918).

65

a more and more familiar sight in the streets of Prague – now had to be taken care of. From 1915 on there was a separate department in the AUVA for these concerns, the "Governmental Central Headquarters for the Kingdom of Bohemia for the Care of Returning Soldiers". But even in peacetime there was no lack of work. He addressed these famous lines to Max Brod for example, who had also secured a "single cycle" job: "In my four districts – aside from my other tasks – people fall off scaffolding like drunks, into machines, all beams tip over, all embankments loosen up and begin to slide, all ladders slip and tumble, whatever one hands up to someone comes crashing down, whatever one hands down, one falls over oneself. And you get a headache from these young girls in porcelain factories who continually throw themselves down the stairs with towering mountains of dishes in their hands."

Kafka's lifelong friend Max Brod (around 1910).

The Neo-Baroque building, crowned with a dome, was built according to the plans of the Prague architect Alfons Wertmüller, who also had a hand in the construction of the New German Theater in Prague. Kafka's office was located on the topmost floor of the building completed in 1896, later on the first floor which also held the office of the president of the company.

In spite of many petitions for leave and for salary increases, Kafka was valued highly by both his colleagues and his superiors and frequently praised. During his twelve-year career in the AUVA he was promoted numerous times, first in 1910 to planner, three years later to vice-secretary, in 1920 to secretary, and 1922, shortly before his retirement, one step further to chief secretary; the last promotion was mainly granted to help the ailing man obtain better social benefits.

THE CAFÉ ARCO IN THE HIBERNERGASSE
Hybernská 16 (II-1004, II-1005)

In the fall of 1907, Josef Suchánek, a café manager from Reichenberg, opened an establishment in the vicinity of the then Prague state railway station which soon became the meeting place of such painters as Max Švabinský, for example. The Arco has become more famous, however, as the coffee house of the Prague German writers, such as Willy Haas, Paul Kornfeld, Hans and Franz Janowitz, Rudolf Fuchs, and Otto Pick. Ernst Weiß, Kurt Tucholsky, and Alfred Kubin also buried themselves in its newspapers, and Johannes Urzidil even made the Arco the scene of his story *Eine Schreckensnacht (A Night of Terror)*, which he incorporated into his swansong for a bygone world in his collection *Die verlorene Geliebte (The Lost Lover)*. The coffee house intellectual from Prague Anton Kuh

View of the interior of the Café Arco in the Hibernergasse (1907).

67

Shifting feelings in the midst of the young people in the Café Arco.

Diary entry by Kafka
on February 25, 1912

characterized the Arco as a "meteorological experimental station for German art and literature": "One could determine from the barometer of the Café 'Arco' exactly when Christian pantheism would begin its dominance, when Expressionism would follow on Impressionism, and which new movement would gather forward momentum." Karl Kraus, the author and publisher of the literary magazine *Die Fackel* *(The Torch)* and known as "Fackel-Kraus", poked fun at the men of letters of the Arco, ennobling them at the same time, when he ironically referred to them as "Arconauts".

Until the onset of his lung disease, Franz Kafka is thought to have belonged to a literary circle in the Arco, where he also made the acquaintance of the Czech journalist Milena Jesenská. Here he also used to make appointments to meet Max Brod, as we can see in a postcard he wrote around the year 1909: "My dear Max – How about coming to the 'Arco' right away for a little while, not for long, God forbid, just to do me a favor, you know, Př. [Příbram] is going to be there. Please gracious Mrs Brod, please Mr Brod, be so kind as to let Max go there. Franz K."

Franz Werfel, the writer of stories, novels, and lyrical poetry is particularly closely linked to the Café Arco. Born in Prague as the son of a well-to-do Jewish industrialist family, he turned to literature at an early age. Even as a pupil in the New Town German High School (Neustädter Deutsches Gymnasium) he was composing poems and plays, and by around 1910 he was considered the center of the Prague "Arco-Circle". From 1912 on he worked as an editor in the Kurt Wolff publishing house in Leipzig. After taking part in the World War he moved to Vienna, where in 1929 he married Gustav Mahler's widow and lived there until the so-called "Anschluß" (annexation of Austria by Nazi

Café „Arco" in Prag
eröffnet.

Germany). In 1938 he had to flee Austria and reached the USA by a circuitous route, where he died after the war of a heart condition.

Kafka made the acquaintance of Werfel through Brod presumably at the end of 1908. His relationship with Werfel subsequently vacillated between admiration and flat rejection. Werfel on the other hand made the crude prophesy about Kafka's work: "That will never get beyond Bodenbach [a provincial city in Bohemia]!" – wrongly as Werfel was forced to realize later. To Felice Bauer Kafka once remarked full of enthusiasm: "Werfel is really a miracle; when I read his book 'Der Weltfreund' [The World's Friend] for the first time (I had previously heard him recite poems) I thought, my enthusiasm for him would carry me away to foolishness. The man can do tremendous things."That Kafka did compete with his very successful writer-colleague can't be dismissed out of hand: "Last Saturday Werfel recited the 'Lebenslieder' [Songs of Life] and the 'Opfer' [Sacrifice]. An enormity! But I looked into his eyes and held his look all evening."

Left: The Prague novelist, dramatist and poet Franz Werfel in a portrait of 1940.

Right: Milena Jesenská (around 1920).

After Werfel's departure Milena Jesenská's husband, Ernst Polak, took on the function of the guiding star at the corner of the Hiberner- and Pflastergasse (Paved Lane), before he too traded the pavement of Prague for that of Vienna.

69

THE PRAGUE ASBESTOS WORKS HERMANN & CO.

Bořivojova 27 (XI-918), Praha-Žižkov

Shortly after his marriage to Elli Kafka on November 27, 1910, Karl Hermann, Kafka's brother-in-law, founded the "Prague Asbestos Works Hermann & Co.", a small factory in the workers' quarter of Žižkov. To this end, a general partnership was applied for at the k. u. k. (Imperial and Royal) Commercial Court in Prague in December 1913. In spite of its impressive sounding name, the "Prague Asbestos Works" seemed at first glance to be more a backyard business than a prospering industrial endeavor. But it was hoped that this would soon change: the production of asbestos and asbestos goods was a promising manufacturing branch at the beginning of the 20th century. The "miracle fiber" was used in the shipping industry, in the building industry, and everywhere a heat and acid resistant insulating material was needed. Such diverse products as automobile tires, stage curtains in theaters, protective clothing for firefighters, and shingles for fire-proof roofs were created from it. The sales of asbestos and asbestos goods climbed steadily; no one spoke of the health risks. Asbestosis, first described as a lung disease in 1900, could not halt the triumphal march of the wondrous fiber.

By founding the "Prague Asbestos Works" Karl Hermann was hopping onto a rolling train, and his father-in-law Hermann Kafka, who wanted to kill two birds with one stone by providing for both his daughter and somewhat dreamy son, recognized the signs of the times. If Franz was not going to follow him into taking over his own business, then he could at least prove himself as a factory owner, at any rate as a secondary occupation. Franz Kafka, himself was perhaps not entirely innocent of the founding of the factory. He must have at least indicated to his father his willingness to participate in its running. Thus, with the financial investment of his father, he became a partner in the "Prague Asbestos Works". Soon, though, all these hopes were blown to the winds. He hated the factory and took part in its management only with great reluctance. The diary entries during these years manifest the torment the asbestos works caused him and give testimony to continuous reproaches from his father and his own feelings of guilt at having once more failed to live up to expectations. He stood around "useless and like a whipped boy" and doubted the possibility of his ever "mastering all the details of the factory's operations." "Miserable factory", he wrote once, when he had had to stand in the engine room for two hours

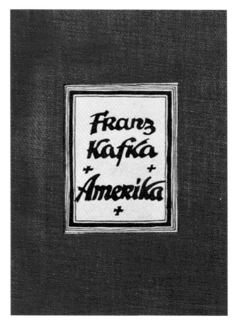

KMEN

LITERÁRNÍ TÝDENNÍK

ROČNÍK IV.   V Praze, dne 22. dubna 1920.   ČÍSLO 6.

Franz Kafka: Topič

Fragment

Se svolenim autorovým přeložila Milena Jesenská

An advertisement for the posthumously published novel *America* in the *Prager Tagblatt* daily paper (1927).

A drawing by Franz Kafka known as "Sitting Man with Drooping Head".

breathing in gas fumes instead of being able to write. All the same, the factory was well equipped with fourteen modern machines and its procedures were for the most part mechanized.

From the very beginning fate bestowed little success on the Prague Asbestos Works, the enterprise functioned inefficiently and continually needed further investments of money. Kafka hated the factory and suffered under the pressure applied by his family who constantly demanded more commitment from him. When he even toyed with the idea of suicide, it became necessary for Max Brod to intervene in order to convince Kafka's mother of the seriousness of the situation. A concerned Julie Kafka was able to talk Paul Hermann, Karl's brother, into standing in for her son – and with that, Franz was out of the hot seat for a while.

Then the First World War broke out and the hours of the factory, in which at one point 25 male and female workers had earned their daily bread, were numbered. When Karl Hermann was drafted into the army, Kafka had to take his turn at the factory again to see to the company's finances. Karl Hermann's brother Paul, who had joined the firm as a third partner back in May 1914, was now in charge of technical management, but could do nothing to prevent its eventual demise. The dearth of raw materials and other essentials, a consequence of the war, did not allow production to continue undisturbed. Thus, in 1917 application was made to liquidate and even before the end of the war in 1918 the Prague Asbestos Works Hermann & Co. was struck from the commercial register. Now Kafka no longer needed to lie on the sofa for hours and think of throwing himself out of the window.

THE CIVILIAN SWIMMING SCHOOL ON THE LESSER TOWN EMBANKMENT OF THE MOLDAU RIVER
U Plovárny 8, Malá Strana

In Kafka's diary under the date August 2, 1914, we find the short, off-hand entry: "Germany declared war on Russia. – Afternoon swimming school". It is one of the frequent mentions of so-called swimming schools that can be found in Kafka's writings about his daily life. Among these establishments were the river swimming facilities not far from Prague in Königsaal and Czernoschitz, the swimming school on the Sophieninsel (Sophie's Island), and the k.u.k. Military Swimming School on the Lesser Town embankment (Kleinseite) of the Moldau near the Kettensteg (Chain Footbridge), which was open not only to military personnel, but also to civilians. This military swimming school had in fact been the first of its kind in Central Europe and was established in 1809. There were also swimming schools on the Schützeninsel (Archers' Island),

The main building of the Prague Civilian Swimming School, in the background the Letná (Belvedere Heights).

73

on the Moldau island of Great-Venice, and in Smíchov. The one that Kafka preferred was the Prague Civilian Swimming School, also called Community Swimming School, a Classicist edifice built in 1840 on the Lesser Town embankment of the Moldau right beneath the Belvedere Heights, which served both swimmers and non-swimmers. Every spring, under the guidance of the swimming supervisors, convicts constructed the wooden platforms for the bathers; after each bathing season the whole structure was dismantled again because of the fear of the ice drifts of winter. It was not the ice, however, that destroyed the facility on one occasion, but rather the floods of 1872: when the wooden platform of the Military Swimming School had broken loose and collided with that of the Civilian Swimming School. In 1875 it was rebuilt and fitted with the modern interior that Kafka knew. There was also a restaurant for refreshments and regular concerts were given for the bathing guests. In a Prague rent by national division, the Civilian Swimming School was counted as a German facility although Czechs frequented it too. The noted merchant Richard Ritter von Dotzauer, one of the founders of the German

Casino and, since 1874, president of the Prague Chamber of Commerce, chaired the society which was in charge of running the recreational facility and saw to it that it retained its German character.

The Swimming School lay within sight of Kafka's parents' apartment in the house "Of the Ship" on the Niklasstraße, only a few steps removed from the Svatopluk Čech Bridge. Even as a young boy Kafka had gone swimming there with his father – how he admired the tall powerful man!

The building of the Civilian Swimming School is still preserved today and serves as a restaurant. The wooden platforms leading down to the river no longer exist.

THE NEW GERMAN THEATER
Wilsonova 4 (II-101), Nové Město

Every evening at seven o'clock, the house curtain rose on the stage of the beautiful theater at 7 Parkstraße (Park Street) – Kafka was there with a student ticket (80 hellers); only a seat up in the gallery was cheaper

The south-western façade of the New German Theater (around 1912).

Ueues deutsches Theater.

Montag den 22. Mai 1899.   Bei aufgehobenem Abonnement.

Anfang 4 Uhr.

(Geburtstag Richard Wagners.)

Richard Wagner-Cyclus
IX.

DIE WALKÜRE.

Erster Tag aus der Trilogie „Der Ring des Nibelungen" in 3 Aufzügen von Richard Wagner.

PERSONEN:

Siegmund · · · Wilhelm Elster   Gerhilde · · · Elle Reid
Hunding · · · Heinrich Wiemer   Ortlinde · · · Helene Eller
Wotan · · · Max Dawison   Waltraute · · · Rita Garnoli
Siegliude · · · Schwertleite · · · Ина Curradini
Brünnhilde · · · Helmine Clant   Helmwige · · · Marie Nagel
Fricka · · · Gisela Matterheim   Siegruue · · · Henriette Heim
                                   Grimgerde · · · Therse Zais
                                   Rossweise · · · Gisela Matterheim

Schauplatz der Handlung:
I. Aufzug: Das Innere der Wohnung Hundings.
II. Aufzug: Wildes Felsengebirg.
III. Aufzug: Auf dem Gipfel eines Felsbergens (des Brünnhildensteins).

Der Beginn der Vorstellung wird durch ein zweimaliges Fanfaren-Signal angezeigt. Das erste, im Foyer, ladet das Publicum ein, sich auf die Plätze zu begeben, das zweite, vor der Bühne, benachrichtiget den Anfang des Actes.

Decorationen, Beleuchtung und Maschinerie eingerichtet von Parcival de Vry, Obermaschinenmeister des Königl. deutschen Landestheaters.

Um Störungen der Gäste, Stellen und Wagslten und zur Originalsänger man in Nachdruck 6 & 7 Uhr. Gnade
Gäste mit Wagslten und zur Nobel im Zeitungs-Schlossen Schweber und 6. Mitte in Delis.

* · Sieglinde · · · · · ·   **Rosa Sucher,**
                              Kgl. Kammersängerin — Berlin.

Beginn des II. Actes 5 Uhr 40 Min., Beginn des III. Actes 7 Uhr 35 Min.

Anfang 4 Uhr.   Ende gegen 9 Uhr.

Gewöhnliche Preise der Plätze.

Kassaeröffn.: Vorv. Eröff. — Tageskasse: Rosa Fuchs.

NEUES DEUTSCHES THEATER.

Dienstag den 23. Mai 1899.   179. Abonn.-Vorst., 2. Serie.

ZAZA.

Schauspiel in 5 Aufzügen von Pierre Berton und Charles Simon. Deutsch von Bolten Baeckers.

Top: A 1899 playbill of the New German Theater attests to the great reverence Prague Germans paid to Richard Wagner.

Top right: The legendary director of the New German Theater: Angelo Neumann (around 1890).

Bottom right: The main entrance of the New German Theater with the approach through the Municipal Park (colorized postcard, around 1907).

(50 hellers). The bourgeoisie of Prague, of course, did not stoop to less than a place in the pit, the stalls, or even a more comfortable seat which cost 6 crowns. And those who felt they owed it to their good name and station would have tried to get a box; those in the circle went for the tidy sum of 24 crowns.

Commissioned by the German Theater Society, the New German Theater was designed by the Viennese theater architects Hermann Helmer and Ferdinand Fellner and built with funds from private foundations and public collections. On the gables of the Classicistic façade one can see the chariot of Dionysus and Thalia; busts of Mozart, Goethe, and Schiller stood underneath the gable until the Second World War. The interior of the theater, especially the auditorium with capacity for two thousand theatergoers, could also compare favorably with the most beautiful opera houses in Europe.

On January 5, 1888, the grand opening of the house was celebrated with a performance of Richard Wagner's *The Mastersingers of Nuremburg (Die Meistersinger von Nürnberg)* and in a few years the stage developed into a launching pad for Austrian and German Bohemian actors and singers. Angelo Neumann, an opera producer in Bremen and a great admirer and pioneering proponent of Wagner, was appointed its director, and in a city with a Czech majority he was able to provide a home for a German theater whose significance was felt beyond its immediate region. Over the years, famous soloists, conductors, and composers contributed greatly to the New German Theater, among them were Leo Blech, Alexander Zemlinsky, Leo Slezak, Richard Tauber, Lotte Lehmann, Maria Jeritza and many others.

76

With the "May Festival", which took place every year from 1899 onwards, Neumann established the first theater festival in Prague, a sort of Bohemian Bayreuth with such international guest stars of the stage and opera as Enrico Caruso. This festival was intended to help tide the theater over summer's off season – and it paid off. Mozart, Beethoven, Mahler, and Verdi's latest compositions were on the program – another frequently recurring name was that of Richard Wagner, who was accorded cult-like reverence in Prague in those days. The director of the theater was good at his job and had an equal gift for self-promotion: "Angelo Neumann's director's box was a stage in itself. In the evening at seven o'clock sharp he

appeared there, a *père noble*, with hair and mustache colored jet black, black suit and tie, and, standing straight, measured the house from top to bottom with a lengthy constant look, then and only then did he give the sign, no, his permission to begin the performance." When Neumann died in 1910, the great days of the May Festivals were numbered, during the World War they were finally shut down completely. Later attempts to renew them did not succeed – German Prague had already lost too much in substance.

Top: Ornaments in the style of German national romanticism (postcard of the *Union of Germans in Bohemia*, around 1910).

Below: The German House on the Graben (around 1910).

THE GERMAN HOUSE AT THE "GRABEN"
Na Příkopě 22 (II-859), Nové Město

The Graben (City Moat) runs between the Powder Tower and the Brückl (the "Little Bridge") at the bottom of Wenceslas Square, an expensive and luxurious shopping street. Even around 1900 this street was probably too lively for someone to walk there immersed in thought; on the other hand the legendary

"corso" took place here every week – a social event among the Prague Germans, where one went to see and be seen, where greeting and being greeted was full of nuances, according to complicated social rules.

The name of the street comes from the water-filled moat which separated the Old Town from the New Town until 1816. In Kafka's time, the moat had long since been covered over and made into an elegant shopping street; here the most expensive stores stood side by side with the most important banks, the most visited coffee houses, and the most exclusive hotels. And here also stood the "German House", a palatial building belonging to the so-called "German Casino" ("Deutsches Kasino") in which hundreds of German societies met and held their celebrations and banquets.

Originally a Baroque structure and rebuilt in the Classicistic style, the building offered large halls for events in addition to an excellent restaurant, a diverse number of rooms for reading and other entertainment, as well as a big garden with a winter garden hall. A series of active societies filled the large house with life, for example, the *Society of German Painters and Sculptors in Bohemia (Verein deutscher bildender Künstler in Böhmen)*, which met every Thursday, or the *German Society for the Dissemination of Knowledge for the Common Good (Deutscher Verein zur Verbreitung gemeinnütziger Kenntnisse)* which annually published a *German People's Calendar* and a series of other entertaining and edifying writings.

With the decline of German liberalism in the 1890s, the significance of the German Casino waned, but the institution still played a prominent role in the cultural and social life in German Prague before the First World War and even continued to do so in the lives of the Germans who stayed on during the First Republic.

Deutsches Haus,

Prag, Graben.

Weltbekanntes größtes Deutsches Restaurant I. Ranges. Ausschank von „Pilsner Urquell", Pschorrbräu, München, österr. EigenbauWeine mit Staatspreis prämiiert. Ausländer Weine erstklassiger Häuser. Bei Versand Spezialpreise. Vorzgl. Küche. Mäss. Preise 43½   Hochachtungsvoll Franz Zoglmann.

An advertisement in the *Prager Tagblatt* extols the "world famous" restaurant with "excellent cuisine" in the German House (1911).

Famous literary figures and poets such as Detlev von Liliencron, Rainer Maria Rilke, Thomas Mann, Bernhard Kellermann, Gerhart Hauptmann, and later also Franz Werfel gave readings from their works in the "Mirror Hall" of the German House.

Prager Tagblatt.

Top: The header of the *Prager Tagblatt.*

Below: A crowd of people
wait for an extra edition of
the *Prager Tagblatt* (presumably in the days following
the assassination of the heir
to the throne Archduke
Franz Ferdinand in Sara-
jevo 1914).

THE EDITORIAL OFFICES
OF THE *PRAGER TAGBLATT*
Panská 8 (II-896), Staré Město

A newspaper read far beyond the borders of Bohemia
was published daily in Prague's Herrengasse – the
Prager Tagblatt (Prague Daily). At first it was only a
paper for advertisements, but soon it printed editorial texts and in its heyday the paper
grew to a size of several dozen pages.

Together with its conservative com-
petitor *Bohemia*, the German liberal
Prager Tagblatt was the newspaper
read in the Kafka family. Son Franz
not only read the *Prager Tagblatt* but
also contributed to it with, for example the story *A Dream (Ein Traum)*
in the morning edition of January 6,
1917, or the story *A Little Woman
(Eine kleine Frau)* in the Easter supplement from 1924. From 1876 to
1938 the paper was a reliable reporter, advertiser of local events, and
cultural guide for the Prague Germans. An army of famous names, odd
fish and originals worked in its offices,
from Egon Erwin Kisch, who earned
his spurs as a journalist by volunteer-

ing there, to Friedrich Torberg, who later published some humorous anecdotes about the newspaper in his book *Tante Jolesch (Aunt Jolesch)*, to Kafka's friend Max Brod, who was a theater and music critic for the *Prager Tagblatt* for many years and set up a monument to his newspaper in the novel *Rebellious Hearts (Rebellische Herzen)*. Thus the legendary figures that peopled the *Prager Tagblatt's* office live on today, such as the editor-in-chief Karl Tschuppik and Dr Siegmund Blau, the latter an early admirer of Kafka, the editor in chief of sports section Dr Raabe-Jenkins, or the regular editorial writer for many years Professor Ludwig Steiner.

Until 1939 the *Prager Tagblatt* was owned by the Prague publishing house Mercy; on the day after German troops marched into Prague the paper became a propaganda tool of the new ruling powers. After the war it could no longer be resurrected.

On June 27, 1924, Hermann and Julie Kafka had an announcement printed in the morning edition of the *Tagblatt*: "Not able to offer our personal thanks individually for the many messages of condolence from near and far we take the liberty to express in this manner our warmest thanks to all those who showed their sympathy at the passing of our unforgettable son Dr Franz Kafka. Family Hermann Kafka."

The composing room of a daily newspaper around 1920.

The weekly supplement of the *Prager Tagblatt* of January 6, 1917, featuring Kafka's short story *A Dream*.

THE CAFÉ SAVOY ON THE
FORMER ZIEGENPLATZ (GOAT SQUARE)
Vězeňská 11 (I-859), Staré Město

Bottom: The building at the former Goat Square that once housed the Café Savoy.

Top right: An advertisement in the *Prager Tagblatt* announces a performance of Jizchak Löwy's theater group at the Café Savoy (1911).

Bottom right: Kafka's Hebrew vocabulary and writing exercises (1911).

As a child Kafka "yawned through" and "dozed through" the hours that he had to spend in the synagogue at his father's side. His deeper interest in questions of Jewish religion and culture was only awakened by the influence of his university friends Hugo Bergmann and Max Brod, avowed Zionists from their youth. He also studied Hebrew intermittently and came into contact with the "Society of Jewish Students" (Bar-Kochba).

Kafka, however, found the academic Zionism of Bar-Kochba less appealing than the folk plays of the Eastern Jewish tradition, which were performed by traveling theater companies in Prague before the First World War. From October 1911 on, after Brod had taken him along to a performance, Kafka regularly attended plays by an Eastern Jewish theater group in the Café Savoy in Prague's Old Town: "14.X.11 Yesterday evening in the Savoy. Sulamit by A. Goldfaden. Actually an opera, but every play that is sung is called operetta …". Soon Kafka knew the texts of the songs by heart and sang along, deeply moved. Yitzhak Löwy, the head and inspiration of the "Yiddish Theater", impressed Kafka greatly and in a short time a friendly relationship developed between the two. Kafka was convinced that he had found an authenticity in the Hasidic Jew from Warsaw which he thought the assimilated western Jews like his father had lost. In the following

82

months he voraciously gobbled up books on Jewish topics and wove Jewish motifs into his own works: "Today began reading the History of the Jews by Grätz greedily and happily."

The Café Savoy on the Ziegenplatz (Goat Square) on the fringes of the old Jewish Quarter was frequented by the everyday people from the surrounding lanes of the Old Town. In 1909, it was taken over by a certain Josef Herrmann and transformed into a night café. The mainly Jewish clientele wasn't bothered by the fact that it still didn't have electric lighting, of more importance was that a morning cup of coffee cost only 24 hellers and that students paid half price. The Jewish theater company from Lemberg was an attraction that enticed many guests there. On Jewish high holidays Herrmann's Café-Restaurant remained closed – that, too, was a concession to its mainly Jewish clientele. The establishment has not withstood the passage of time.

THE OLD-NEW SYNAGOGUE
Červená, Staré Město

Jews are said to have lived in Prague from time immemorial, pious settlers, of whom nothing remains but the buried ruins of an old temple. At the close of the Middle Ages, building workers stumbled across these remains as they were about to dig the foundations of a new synagogue – according to legend, at least. Thus, the name "Old-New Synagogue" suggested itself quite obviously. Built on such firm ground, the temple lasted through the centuries, and remained standing tall into the Prague sky even when various conflagrations reduced the surrounding houses of the Jewish Quarter to ash and rubble. Therefore, even today Jews from

Kafka went to nearly twenty performances by this Galician theater group and over and above that he promoted the "Lemberger" (actors from the Galician city of Lemberg) by seeing to it that they got publicity in articles in the Prager Tagblatt (by way of Max Brod) or also in the the Jewish weekly Selbstwehr (Self Defense), or by helping them get guest performances in the provincial towns of Bohemia.

The former Jewish Quarter after the sanation. To the left the new, elegant houses of Niklasstraße, to the right the Old-New Synagogue and the Jewish Town Hall with its clock tower (around 1910).

all over the world assemble in the "Great Synagogue" beneath Hebrew inscriptions and Bible verses to repeat the Jewish creed: "Schema Israel …"

The Old-New Synagogue was built at the end of the 13th century: stone masons from the royal mason's lodge built the walls and vaulted the ceiling of the synagogue. Two columns were to lend its two naves support and strength, and twelve windows with pointed arches reminded the believers of the twelve Jewish tribes. In the middle of the inner chamber divided by the two columns stands the Almemor, a type of rostrum from which the Torah is read aloud to the assembled community and sermons are delivered. An iron lattice surrounds the altar-space under a large candelabrum with nine branches, and set in the east wall is the Aron Hakodesh, the ark in which parchment rolls containing the five Books of Moses are kept.

An entrance hall was added to the original building in the 14th century, in which the two collection boxes of the tax collectors were anchored. The tympanum decorations above the portal stem from the same period and symbolize the vine with the twelve

tribes of Israel. Later, in the 15th century, the characteristic brick gable was set in front of the edifice, and only in the 18th century was the side nave added so that women, too, could follow the religious services in the main hall. Orthodox Jewish women were only allowed to set foot in the synagogue once in their lives – on the day of their marriage.

In a diary note from October 1911 Kafka allows us to take part in the solemn atmosphere in the Old-New Synagogue on a holy day: "Old-New Synagogue yesterday. Kol Nidre. Dampened stock-exchange-mumbling. In the entry hall a box with the inscription: 'Mild gifts, quietly given, calm reluctance.' Churchlike interior. Three pious obviously Eastern Jews. In stocking feet. Bent over their prayer books, their prayer shawls pulled over their heads, having become as small as possible. Two of them are crying, moved by just the holy day? One of them perhaps only has eyes that hurt, onto which he fleetingly presses his still folded sack cloth only to hold his face up close to the text again. The word isn't actually or not primarily sung, but following the word, arabesques are drawn out of the word which is spun out thin as a hair. The small boy, who without the least idea of the whole ceremony, without any possibility of orientating himself, the noise in his ears, squeezes himself in between the people standing close together and is pushed by them. What seems to be a clerk, who, while praying, gives himself a quick shake, which can only be understood as an attempt at the strongest possible, but perhaps also most incomprehensible emphasis of every word, in which the voice is spared, a voice moreover that in all this noise could not bring about a clear and resounding emphasis. The family of the brothel owner. In the Pinkas Synagogue I was incomparably more moved by Judaism."

A view of the prayer room in the Old-New Synagogue with its Gothic vaults (around 1870).

THE JEWISH TOWN HALL
Maiselova 18 (V-250), Staré Město

Opposite the Old-New Synagogue stands the Jewish Town Hall, purchased by the Jewish community in 1577. The Italian master builder Pankraz Roder was entrusted by the Jewish City fathers with the necessary alterations as well as with the addition of a New Town Hall Synagogue (also called the High Synagogue). The money for this construction was given by Mordechai Maisel, the rich banker of the Jewish Quarter and the benefactor of Prague's Jews. Here, in the immediate neighborhood of the Old-New Synagogue and of the kosher slaughter houses, the real center of the Jewish Quarter developed over time.

The Jewish Town Hall seen from the former Rabbinergasse (today's Maiselová, around 1910).

The history of the Jewish Town Hall reflects the mixed fortunes of the Prague Jews. After Prague was

Redaktion,
Administration u. Expedition
Prag II., Soukenická 34.

Postsparkassenkonto 90.129.

Telephon Nr. 467/VIII.

Sprechstunde der Redaktion
11—12 Uhr vormittags.

Redaktionsschluß
Mittwoch 9 Uhr vorm.

Erscheint jeden Freitag.

Selbstwehr

Unabhängige jüdische Wochenschrift.

Abonnement m. Postzusend
Ganzjährig K 20.—, halb
K 10.—, vierteljähr. K 5.—
Für Deutschland Mk. 15.—
Für das übrige Ausland
15 Frcs. oder 15 sh.

Einzelne Nummer 40 Heller.

Insertionspreis:
Die sechsmal gespalt. Petitzeile
oder deren Raum 50 Heller.
Inseratenannahme durch die
Annoncen-Bureaus und die
Administration.

XIII. Jahrgang.   Prag, den 3. Jänner 1919.   Nr. 1.

Der Jüdische Nationalrat bei Präsident Masaryk.

Der Präsident der tschechoslowakischen Republik Th. G. Masaryk empfing am 31. De- chen Bestands der jüdischen Nation im tsche- dischen Staate gefordert und weiters der tsche- hinwies, daß den ersten Schritt zur Lösung aller dieser brennenden Fragen die rechtliche,

besieged by the Swedes in 1648 the authorities allowed the Jews to build a tower for the town hall in gratitude for their help in the defense of the city. During the great fire in the Old Town in 1682 the town hall was heavily damaged, but was successfully repaired afterward by the architect Paul Ignaz Bayer. Then, Empress Maria Theresia issued an edict banning all Jews from the city and they were forced to leave with bag and baggage. The banishment was destined to be short-lived, but when the Prague Jews had re-established themselves in the Jewish Quarter, the proud town hall fell victim to conflagration once again. The necessary rebuilding and repair work was carried out between 1763 and 1765 in the Rococo style. At that time the Jewish Town Hall received its present day appearance, and the High Synagogue was separated from the town hall. A wooden tower was placed on the roof with two clocks from the workshop of the royal court watchmaker Sebastian Landesberger, the first indicating the time in Latin, the second in Hebraic numbers. In the course of the "sanation" toward the close of the 19th century, the Jewish Town Hall was almost demolished. Eventually, however, it was agreed that the historic edifice

An edition of *Selbstwehr* *("Self-Defense")* of January 3, 1919. Max Brod and Franz Kafka were not only avid readers of the Zionist weekly, but also contributed texts.

The Jewish Town Hall during the demolition works in the course of the sanation (postcard after an oil painting by Jan Minařík of 1906).

should be integrated into a new building. This south-facing extension, which in fact replaced a whole terrace of old houses, was officially opened in 1909.

The seat of the "Council of the Jewish Cultural Community", a ritual dining hall, and the offices of the Prague Jewish Community are presently located in the town hall. The High Synagogue has become one of the venues of the Jewish Museum.

On February 18, 1912, Franz Kafka arranged an evening of recitations with his friend Yitzhak Löwy's theater group, Kafka himself introduced the evening with a short talk on the Yiddish jargon.

The Hotel "Archduke Stephen" ("Erzherzog Stephan")

Václavské náměstí 25 (II-825), Nové Město

In 1846, the innkeeper of the "Schweinhäusel" ("Little Pighouse") on Wenceslas Square, a simple beer-pub that was nevertheless often sought out by elegant guests, was granted permission by the General-Viceroy of Bohemia Archduke Stephen, who also dropped in there on occasion, to ennoble the inn with his name. The change of name must have done the establishment much good: the hotel flourished as did all of Wenceslas Square, increasingly becoming a modern metropolitan boulevard. Around 1903, the Hotel "Archduke Stephen" was equipped with the most modern technical appointments of the times and re-opened as a prestigious Art Nouveau hotel. In 1911, it was advertised as the "biggest and most modern" hotel in the city, pointing out its 130 rooms and salons, electric lighting, central heating, elevator and telephone, both "metropolitan and interurban". In the intoxication brought on by victory after the First World War – archdukes were now frowned upon – a new sign was affixed over the wide balcony on the face of the hotel: *Hotel President Woodrow Wilson*. In the end, however, it was named after its owner: *Grand Hotel Šroubek*. After the Second World War, the communist rulers changed the "bourgeois" name to the one it still carries today, *Hotel Evropa*.

In 1912, the "Johann-Gottfried-Herder-Society" sent out invitations to an author reading on December 4, under the direction of Willy Haas

Commercial postcard of the Hotel "Archduke Stephen" (1911/1912).

and to take place in the mirror hall of the Hotel "Archduke Stephen". First on the program were poems by Franz Werfel and Otto Pick, followed by excerpts from works by Max Brod and Oskar Baum. Kafka, still hardly known in literary circles, was slated to provide the grand finale with his reading of his story *The Judgment (Das Urteil)*, for which he needed a little less than thirty minutes. It was the first and only public reading from his work in Prague. Immediately afterwards he wrote to Felice Bauer: "Every other evening is more important than the one today, which only served for my entertainment, whereas the other evenings are meant for my liberation. Dearest, I really take devilish pleasure in reading aloud, to bellow into the prepared and attentive ears of the listeners

The café in the Hotel "Archduke Stephen" (around 1911).

does my poor heart so good. And I really gave them a good earful and just blew away the music from neighboring rooms that wanted to relieve me of the burden of reading. You know, ordering people about or at least believing in one's power of command – there is no greater comfort for the body." Kafka had completed *The Judgment* in September 1912 in the course of one single night. That was shortly after his first encounter with Felice Bauer, to whom it is also dedicated and who shared the initials of Frieda Brandenfeld, the fiancée of the protagonist in this story.

The story of the young businessman George Bendemann was the start of a series of accomplished works, and the stylistic perfection it attained was to become Kafka's guideline for all his further works. In 1913 the story appeared in the yearbook of poetic art *Arkadia* in Leipzig and three years later it was published as a separate volume by the publishing house of Kurt Wolff.

Franz Kafka (1910).

THE APARTMENT OF MAX BROD'S PARENTS IN THE SCHALENGASSE (SHELL LANE)
Skořepka 1 (I-527), Staré Město

Until 1913, Kafka's friend Max Brod, then a post office official and literature-loving bachelor, lived together with his parents and his brother Otto in an apartment in the Old Town's Schalengasse (Shell Lane). Adolf Brod, his father, occupied a senior position as director of the Union Bank in Prague.

On August 13, 1912, after 9 o'clock in the evening, Kafka visited Max Brod in order to select, with his advice, the texts for his first prose collection *Meditation (Betrachtung)*. On this evening a young woman from Berlin named Felice Bauer was present, with

Together with his parents and his brother Otto, Max Brod lived on the top floor at No 1 Schalengasse. Here Felice Bauer and Franz Kafka met for the first time (picture around 1900).

whom Kafka soon entered into conversation. A few days later he confided to his diary: "Fräulein Felice Bauer. When I came to Brod's apartment on 13th VIII she was sitting at the table and yet seemed to me like a servant girl. And I wasn't curious at all who she was, but accepted her presence there immediately. Bony empty face that openly showed off its emptiness. Neck free. Blouse hastily thrown over her. Looked as if pretty homely dressed, although she was not at all homely, as became evident later on. … Almost broken-looking nose. Blonde, somewhat stiff unattractive hair, prominent chin. While I was sitting down, I took my first more precise look at her, as soon as I had sat down, I already had made an irrevocable judgment about her."

Following that, the couple exchanged innumerable letters – more than five hundred by Kafka alone have been preserved. And although they saw each other seldom, they were engaged twice, without, however, ever getting married and founding a household. The capable fiancée was employed in a good position in the firm of Carl Lindström, which manufactured dictation machines and the so-called "Parlograph" – and thus had little time for, and probably also little interest in, literature. For his part, Kafka complained continually that he was incapable of submitting to the yoke of marriage, that he was frightened away by middle class conventions and that a marriage would be detrimental to his writing. While

Felice later started a family, Kafka stayed a bachelor until the end of his days.

The corner house on the top floor of which Max Brod's parents' apartment was situated was a new construction from the 1880s. The Czech architect Antonín Wiehl and the builder Karel Gemperl had built it as an elegant apartment house in the style of the Czech Neo-Renaissance in the Old Town. Three stories with a façade made of clinker rise above the ground floor; on the corner we find an oriel (a large decorative bay window). The top floor underneath the gable is decorated with sgraffiti whose motifs are borrowed from the Czech painter Mikoláš Aleš' imaginary world.

Max Brod in a caricature of 1909.

Before the outbreak of the First World War Max Brod and his wife set up their own household, initially at 1 Bischofsgasse (Bishop's Lane) (II-1065), then, from February 1914, at 3/13 Elišky Krásnohorské Street (I-897) opposite the Church of the Holy Spirit (Heiliggeistkirche) in the Old Town. There, too, Kafka was among the guests, as a diary entry of February 14, 1914, tells us. In September 1914, the Brods moved into what was to become their home for the next two decades, the elegant apartment dwelling at No 8 Ufergasse (Embankment Lane) (V-208) in the area that had once been the old Jewish Quarter. It was not until August 1938 that the Brod family moved on to 8 Bischofshof (Bishop's Court) (II-1147). From here they embarked on their emigration on March 14, 1939, one day before Prague was occupied by German troops.

Engagement portrait of Felice Bauer and Franz Kafka (1917).

THE OPPELT-HOUSE ON THE OLD TOWN SQUARE
Staroměstské náměstí 5 (I-934), Staré Město

From November 1913 on, the Kafka family lived in the uppermost floor of the "Oppelt-House", a Neo-Baroque apartment house from the turn of the 20th century. The family rented the flat until 1932; for about four years from 1920, Kafka's sister Ottla and her husband Josef David lived on the floor below the parental apartment. In the wake of the battles fought around the Old Town Hall in 1945, the house was heavily damaged and was rebuilt in 1946 one floor shorter. Thus the apartment the Kafkas lived in is no longer in existence.

From his room Kafka could look down on the elegant Niklasstraße: "I have, by the way, a beautiful

view, which you can perhaps imagine on occasion, if your good feeling for topography is matched by
an equally good memory. Straight
ahead from my window on the 4ᵗʰ
or 5ᵗʰ floor I have the great cupola
of the Russian Church with two
towers, and between the cupola and
the next apartment building a little
triangular cut-out view of the Laurenziberg (Mount St Lawrence) with
a very small church on it. To the left
I see the Town Hall with its tower
in all its bulk rising up sharply and
laying itself back, in a perspective
that no person has perhaps really
seen yet."

In his later years, already marked
by his lung disease, Kafka returned
into the care of his parents who were
still living in the Oppelt-House.
Since Ottla was in Zürau and later
attended an agricultural college in
Friedland, Kafka was able to live in
her room: "Your bedroom is not a
bedroom. I won't say anything
about the kitchen, nothing about
the courtyard, at ½ 6 it's noisy, that
is all a matter of course, even if
today is Sunday. By the way, not
even the cat could be heard, just the
clock in the kitchen. But above all
the bathroom. Three times according to my count the light was turned
on there and water was turned on
for incomprehensible purposes, then
added to all that the door to the bedroom was left open so that I heard
Father coughing. Poor Father, poor
Mother, poor Franz."

The Flat in the Bílekgasse (Bílek Lane)

Bílkova 10 (I-868), Staré Město

Finally rented a room. In the same house in the Bílekgasse.

Diary entry by Kafka on February 9, 1915

The tenement building at Bílekgasse in which Franz Kafka twice made his home.

In the summer of 1914 Kafka's brother-in-law Karl Hermann was called up for military service. Consequently, his wife, Kafka's sister Elli, sought refuge in the parental apartment in the Oppelt-House along with her two young children. Since there was not enough space for all of them, Kafka moved out – of benefit to all concerned. He was able to stay for a month at his sister Valli's in Bílek Lane.

In February and March 1915, Kafka returned to live in the same house in Bílek Lane, this time, however, as the principal tenant of a small flat. Right away on the first evening Kafka's peace and quiet was disturbed, because his neighbor conversed for hours with the landlady: "Both speak softly, the landlady almost inaudible, so much the worse. My writing, which had finally picked up 2 days ago, interrupted, who knows for how long. Pure desperation. Is it going to be that way in every apartment? Is such a ridiculous and certainly deadly adversity in store for me with every landlady in every city?" And it continued in the same vein: "Everything stalled. Bad irregular budgeting of time. The apartment spoils everything for me. Listened again today to the landlady's daughter's French lesson." On March 1, 1915, Kafka finally gave notice that he was moving out, after "weeklong preparations and fear" and "from my own disquiet".

THE HOUSE "OF THE GOLDEN PIKE" ("ZUM GOL-DENEN HECHT") IN THE LANGE GASSE (LONG LANE)

Dlouhá 16 (I-705), Staré Město

On March 15, 1915, Kafka moved into new living quarters: "A comfortable friendly corner room, two windows, a balcony door. View out onto many roofs and churches. Tolerable people, since with some practice I don't have to see them. Noisy street, heavy vehicles in the earliest part of the morning, which I have almost grown used to. The room, however, uninhabitable for me. Although it does lie at the end of a long antechamber and is outwardly isolated enough, it is a concrete house; I hear, that is, I heard, the sighs of the neighbors, the conversations of the people living below, here and there a bang from the kitchen even long after 10 p.m.. Besides, above the thin ceiling of the room there was the attic, and one could never know on which late afternoon, just when I wanted to work, a servant girl hanging up the washing wouldn't positively, in complete innocence, kick my skull in with the heel of her little boot. Now and then there was also piano playing and in summer from the semicircle of the other encroaching houses singing, a violin and a gramophone. Anything approximating silence only from 11 o'clock at night on. So, impossibility to gain peace, complete homelessness, breeding place of insanity, increasingly greater weakness and hopelessness."

The house "Of the Golden Pike", in which Kafka lived for nearly two years.

97

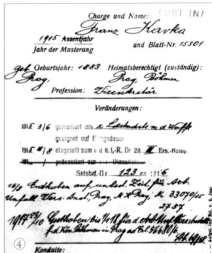

He was to remain in his quarters until the end of February 1917; these were sublet from a Mr Salomon Stein on the fifth floor of the house "Of the Golden Pike", a newly constructed building in Prague's Old Town. An attractive house, a much friendlier room than the one in Bílek Lane, about 30 square meters in size, a balcony, and a view of the Tein Church – if only there hadn't been the incessant noise and, from time to time, a rumbling above the kitchen which resembled "a rolling ball like in a game of ninepins"! "I moved into a room in which the noise is around ten times greater than in the previous one, but which is otherwise incomparably nicer. I thought myself to be detached from the location and the appearance of the room. But I'm not. Without a freer view, without the possibility of seeing a big piece of sky out of the window and possibly a tower in the distance, even if it can't be open countryside, without this I am a miserable, depressed person; although I can't pin down what part of my misery is on account of the room, it can't be small; I even have the morning sun in my room and since there are much lower roofs around, the sunshine comes fully and straight away to me. But I don't only have the morning sun, because it is a corner room and two windows look out to the southwest. But so I don't get too high spirited, somebody above me in a (empty, unrented!) studio tramps back and forth in boots and has set up some kind of useless noise-machine there that gives the illusion of a game of ninepins. A heavy ball, thrown quickly, rolls the full length of the ceiling of the room, strikes in the corner and rolls back with a dull roar." Of course, it wasn't heavy boots or some useless apparatus, but the machinery of an elevator: "In my room, of course, all hell breaks loose; behind the right wall logs are apparently being stacked, one hears how a trunk is loosened from the wagon, then it is raised, it sighs like a living thing, then a crash, it falls and the resonance of the whole cursed concrete house absorbs it. Above the room in the attic the machinery

The World War 1914–18:

Image 1: "Firm and True": The emperors Franz Joseph and Wilhelm II as loyal allies on a postcard of 1914.

Image 2: Cadets of the Army Supply Train School of Prague (1910). The building houses the Ministry of Defense today.

Image 3: The model trench in Prague was a popular place of interest. Kafka was among the many visitors who sought a glimpse at the life in the front line.

Image 4: Kafka's military record of 1915 shows him fit for service, but working in a reserved occupation at the AUVA.

Image 5: Poster by Julius Klinger advertising the eighth war bond (1918). Kafka had signed war bonds himself and was hoping for the ultimate victory of the Central Powers.

Image 6: The real war: a German trench in 1914.

I don't have any time. General mobilization is taking place. K[arl Hermann] and P[aul Hermann] have been called up. Now I receive the reward for being alone.

Diary entry by Kafka at the end of July, 1914

of the elevator drones and reverberates through the empty attic space. (That is the studio ghost I supposed earlier; there is, however, also a servant girl who, while hanging up the laundry to dry, positively gropes her way over the top of my cranium with her wooden clogs.)"

The Secessionist-style apartment building "Of the Golden Pike" was erected in the years 1911–1914 by the Czech architect Karel Janda on the site of two earlier buildings, originating in the 15th century, which were cleared in the course of the sanation of the Old Town: these houses were the original "Of the Golden Pike" and "Of the Golden Cow". The architectural plans give evidence of the studio Kafka mentioned and the elevators he complained about. During Kafka's time there were a pub and a printing shop on the ground floor of the building.

THE LITTLE COTTAGE IN THE GOLDEN LANE
Zlatá ulička 22 (IV-20), Pražský hrad

Probably one of the best-known Kafka sites is the little cottage at No 22 Golden Lane in the Prague Castle complex. The lane, a blind alley at both ends, also called Alchemists' Lane or Goldmakers' Lane, was laid out at the end of the 16th century. In 1594, Emperor Rudolf II permitted 24 "marksmen before the gates of the Prague Castle" to build a settlement in the recesses of the northern fortress wall. Village life must have soon developed there, since the inhabitants built small stalls and pens to house small animals, let chickens scratch around in the mud and transformed the street into a sort of sewer. It wasn't until the 19th century that conditions improved and the narrow lane took on its present appearance. Under pressure from the castle administration the last inhabitants had to leave the lane in the 1950s.

It was to this picturesque spot that Kafka and his sister had gone around the middle of 1916 to find a

In my room I am sitting in the head-quarters of noise.

Kafka jotted down this line in his diary on November 5, 1911. He subsequently used it as the opening of a prose sketch entitled "Great Noise", which was published in the *Herder-Blätter* literary journal in October 1912.

Left: Franz Kafka at the age of 31 (1914).

101

retreat for writing: "Once in summer I went with Ottla to search for a flat; I no longer believed in the possibility of real peace and quiet, nevertheless I went looking. We saw several things in the Lesser Town, all the while I thought, if only there were some little hole somewhere in an attic corner, in order to stretch out in peace there. We found nothing, nothing to speak of really. Just for fun we inquired in the small lane. Yes, a small house would be available to rent in November. Ottla, who was also looking for quiet, but in her way, fell in love with the thought of renting the house. I, in my inbred weakness, advised against it. That I could be there too, I hardly imagined. So small, so dirty, so uninhabitable, with all imaginable deficiencies. She insisted on it, however, had it completely whitewashed when the big family that was living there had been moved out, bought a few pieces of cane furniture (I know of no more comfortable chair than this), kept it, and keeps it, a secret from the rest of the family. ... It had many initial drawbacks; I don't have enough time to tell of the development. Today it suits me completely.

Top: The little cottage at No 22 Golden Lane that Kafka used as a retreat.

Left: The Golden Lane (colorized postcard, 1910).

Only seldom did friends come, perhaps Oskar Baum or in February, 1917, Max Brod, who wrote in his diary afterwards: "At Kafka's in the Alchemists' Lane. He reads aloud beautifully. The monk's cell of a real poet."

103

In every way: the beautiful path leading up, the silence there, only a thin wall separates me from a neighbor, but that neighbor is quiet enough; I carry my supper up there and usually stay until midnight; then the advantage of the way home: I have to decide to stop working, I then have a walk that will cool my head. And life there: it's something special to have one's own house, to lock the door on the world, not the door of a room, not that of an apartment, but actually the door of a house, to step out the door of your living quarters into the snow in the silent street. The whole thing twenty crowns per month, furnished by my sister with everything necessary, looked after as little as needs be by the little flower girl, everything in order and nice."

One couldn't imagine a more suitable place to write: a small living room, all in all hardly more than fifteen square meters, a small window looking out onto the green Hirschgraben (Stag Moat), another one over the lane, between the entrance door and the living room a tiny vestibule with just enough room for two passages leading through, one up to the attic, the other over stone steps into the cellar

I was in a dire predicament: an urgent journey lay before me; a gravely ill patient awaited me in a village ten miles away; a heavy snowfall filled the vast space between me and him …

The opening of the short story *A Country Doctor*

vault. Down there the castle administration had an exhibition alchemist's laboratory set up in the fifties with a fireplace, pipettes, glass flasks and similar things; this was after the previous owner Anežka Michlová, born Sofrová, then a 46-year-old laundry woman and kitchen assistant in the Lobkowicz Palace, had been forced to sell the small property, which was already valuable even then. Originally, only the little house at number 20 had belonged to her, but when she, a widow herself, married the widower and lithographer to the regional court Bohumil Michl during the First World War, she also became the owner of number 22, which she was able to rent to Ottla. From May 1917

Left: Kafka with his sister Ottla, who was one of his most intimate confidantes.

on Mr and Mrs Michl lived in house number 20, immediately next door to Kafka.

Kafka usually spent the evening hours in the tiny little house, after he had done his day's work and also taken his supper. He could not stay in the small, ill-equipped room, however. Thus he usually went away in the early morning hours or toward "midnight down to the city by way of the Alte Schloßstiege [Old Castle Stairs]" and struck out over the then still new Archduke Franz Ferdinand Bridge (also called the "New Bridge" by the Prague Germans, renamed Mánes-Bridge after April 1920) and through the Karpfengasse to his apartment in the Lange Gasse.

In this house in the Alchemists' Lane a whole series of prose pieces and fragments came into existence from the late fall of 1916 on, among them were almost all the stories that appeared in 1920 in the collection *A Country Doctor (Ein Landarzt)*. The Kurt Wolff Publishing House published the volume "192 pages big octavo-size in particularly elegant lay-out" and beat the advertising drum for the book. But Kafka's name was still only known to a small, dedicated group of readers, and so successful sales figures remained absent: "proof against the reading public", as a reviewer stated very succinctly.

In the summer of 1917 the owner Anežka Michlová revoked the lease, which hardly perturbed the occupant whose tuberculosis had just come to light: "But better this way, perhaps I couldn't have been in the damp little house at all".

THE SCHÖNBORN PALACE IN THE LESSER TOWN (KLEINSEITE)
Tržiště 15 (III-365), Malá Strana

In March 1917 Kafka rented a two-room flat in the Schönborn Palace in the Lesser Town (Kleinseite), big enough for himself and, if necessary, also for his bride Felice. Of course, it was only a cold, stuffy, and bad smelling apartment, but nonetheless it was in the best location and moreover completely quiet. To get it he had given notice on his living quarters in the Lange Gasse. The palace had been rebuilt around the middle of the 17th century by the then owner, the

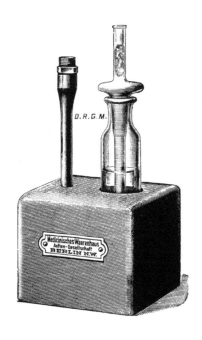

D.R.G.M.

Medicinisches Waarenhaus
Actien-Gesellschaft
BERLIN N.W.

Top right: Instruments for the diagnosis of tuberculosis (around 1910).

Top right: Cover detail of Franz Kafkas collection of short stories *A Hunger Artist* (1924).

Bottom right: The diagnosis and discharge paper of Kafka from the Viennese Laryngological Hospital, April 19, 1924.

Grand Prior of the Order of Malta Rudolf Colloredo-Waldsee, in the Early Baroque manner; in 1794 it became the property of the Counts of Schönborn. Today it houses the United States of America's ambassadorial headquarters in the Czech Republic and instead of tranquil peacefulness, a constant coming and going prevails, and even harmless passers-by are eyed suspiciously by the security personnel. In Kafka's days, however, the so-called Lesser Town Vegetable Market extended out in front of it, a street market with a most varied collection of vegetable stands which reached down to the Karmelitergasse (Carmelites' Lane). What a paradise for the vegetarian Kafka!

Kafka had just half-way become settled down in the Schönborn Palace, when in the night of August 12 to 13, he suffered a lung hemorrhage. Already earlier that month he had coughed up some blood while swimming in the Civilian Swimming School, but had refused to recognize anything disturbing in that. Now there were no doubts anymore as to the nature or the gravity of his illness – tuberculosis. Kafka later described the nocturnal occurrence to his mistress Milena: "About 3 years ago it began in the middle of the night with a hemorrhage. I got up, perturbed as one is by everything new (instead of remaining lying down, as I later learned one should do), naturally somewhat startled, walked around in the room, went to the window, leaned out, went to the washstand, walked around in the room, sat down on the bed – continually blood. At the same time I was not unhappy, because it dawned on me for a specific reason that after 3, 4 sleepless years – assuming that the bleeding stopped – I would be able to sleep for the first time. And it stopped (hasn't appeared again since then) and I slept the rest of the night. In the morning, however, the maid came (at that time I had an apartment in the Schönborn Palace), a good, very devoted, but extremely matter-of-fact girl, saw the blood and said: 'Pane doktore, s Vámi to dlouho nepotrvá.' ['Doctor, you're not going to last much longer.'] But I felt better than usual, I went to the office and to the doctor only in the afternoon. The further story is immaterial here."

Dr Gustav Mühlstein, the family doctor whom he soon contacted, diagnosed bronchial catarrh. On the advice of Max Brod, Kafka also had himself examined by a lung specialist, although he had already come up with his own interpretation of the illness: "It was this way: the brain couldn't bear the cares and pain that had been inflicted on it any longer. It said: 'I give up; if there is anyone here who is still interested in maintaining the whole body, then he should relieve me of some of my burden and it can continue a little while longer.' That's when the lung reported for duty."

MUDr Friedel Pick, professor of internal medicine and director of the laryngological institute of the German University of Prague, finally confirmed the suspicion: catarrh of the outer lobe of the lungs. Kafka's comment: "that's like saying piggy when you really mean fat sow".

Soon Kafka learned that there might be also some bright sides to consumption, for example when it came to running away from his engagement with Felice once again. Tuberculosis – that was not only the curse of Job, but also an opportunity for early retirement. Without hesitation, Kafka applied for it on September 6, 1917, at first, admittedly, without success. All the same, he was granted a three month vacation to recuperate, which he wanted to spend in the idyllic countryside with his sister in Zürau. At this time Kafka gave up his domicile in the Schönborn Palace: "Dear Ottla, well, I've moved out. I closed the windows in the palace for the last time, locked the door, how similar that must be to dying."

THE NEW JEWISH CEMETERY IN PRAGUE
Nad vodovodem 1, Strašnice

In the end, Kafka could only communicate by means of notes written on slips of paper, as he waited for death in Kierling near Klosterneuburg, racked by pain and tormenting thirst. On one of these scraps was written: "Kill me or else you are a murderer." In the morning of June 3, 1924, Kafka died, nursed to the end by his lover Dora Diamant and his friend Robert Klopstock.

Kafka's death notice in the *Prager Tagblatt* (1924).

In tiefstem Schmerz geben wir bekannt, daß unser Sohn

JUDr. Franz Kafka

am 3. Juni im Sanatorium Kierling bei Wien, 41 Jahre alt, gestorben ist. Das Begräbnis findet am Mittwoch, den 11. Juni um ³/₄4 Uhr auf dem jüdischen Friedhof in Straschnitz statt.

PRAG, am 10. Juni 1924.

Hermann und **Julie Kafka,**
Eltern,
3392   im Namen der trauernden Hinterbliebenen.

Von Kondolenzbesuchen bitten wir abzusehen.

After an intervention by official doctors his body was turned over to the City Funeral Services of the Community of Vienna and transferred to Prague in a sealed metal casket. Eight days after Kafka's passing, on June 11, 1924, his burial took place in dull gray weather at the New Jewish Cemetery in Prague-Strašnice. His family, friends, and acquaintances, the last love of his life, Dora Diamant, in addition to a community of mourners made up of Czech, German, and Jewish admirers of the writer followed the casket. While Hebrew prayers were recited Kafka's simple wooden coffin was lowered into the grave.

The ceremonial hall of the New Jewish Cemetery.

The New Jewish Cemetery, laid out in the late 19th century and originally designed for 100,000 gravesites, was one of the biggest cemeteries in Prague. The grounds include the Ceremonial Hall in the style of the Neo-Renaissance with a prayer chamber, as well as an administration building at the entrance. Important architects of the turn of the last century, among them Antonín Balšánek, Jan Kotěra, Josef Fanta, Čeněk Vosmík, and Josef Zasche designed many of the cemetery's splendid tombstones; a walk through their rows is like a walk through a sunken world. Among the graves of rich Jewish factory owners and burghers of the late 19th century are the last resting places of such luminaries of Prague's intellectual life as: the writers Ota Pavel and Oskar Baum, the painter Max Horb, the philosopher Vilém Flusser, and, in the grove of urns,

111

the ashes of the Czech poet Jiří Orten.

Kafka's grave is located about 200 meters removed from the custodian's house, right across from the cemetery wall. The author's parents, Julie and Hermann, have also been interred here. The Prague architect Leopold Ehrmann designed the slender cubist gravestone in the form of a hexagonal crystal cut off at the bottom. It carries a Hebrew inscription which translated into English says: "Dr Franz Kafka, 1883–1924, Tuesday, at the beginning of the month Siwan 5684. The magnificent, unmarried man, cited above, our teacher and Master Anschel, of blessed memory, is the son of the greatly revered R. Henoch Kafka, may his light shine. His mother's name is Jettl. May his soul be bound in the union of life!" The memorial tablet set up against the stone is of a newer date and commemorates the fate of Kafka's sisters, all of whom perished in concentration camps.

Opposite the gravesite with the grave number 21-14-21, the Jewish Cultural Community in Prague has set a memorial plaque to Max Brod into the cemetery wall – honoring the "Writer and thinker, pioneer of Czech culture abroad, friend of Franz Kafka, and editor of his works".

THE FRANZ-KAFKA-MONUMENT
Vězeňská, Staré Město

It took almost eighty years until a monument was erected to Franz Kafka in his native city of Prague: On December 4, 2003, on the occasion of Kafka's 120th birthday, the local Franz Kafka Society unveiled a cast-bronze statue 3.75 meters high, weighing 700 kilograms. Hundreds of Kafka enthusiasts took part in the celebration, among them not a few in black suits, hats, and coats.

Its location was carefully chosen: a small plateau between the Church of the Holy Spirit (Heiliggeistkirche) and the Spanish Synagogue, at the entrance of the former Jewish Quarter. Thus, since that date a roguish Kafka-figure has ridden on the shoulders of a man's form which has been reduced to a headless, armless, footless, empty suit of clothes. The young Czech sculptor Jaroslav Róna hit upon this subject, so the newspapers reported, while reading Kafka's *Description of a Struggle (Beschreibung eines Kampfes)*.

In spite of continual discussions and negative critiques, his monument to Kafka made Jaroslav Róna famous beyond the borders of the Czech Republic. The many tourists who have themselves photographed in all possible poses in front of the statue appear to like it. And sooner or later the grumbling, fault-finding Prague burghers will get used to this new postcard image standing in their Old Town.

Top left: Franz Kafka's tombstone (taken before 1947).
Bottom left: The memorial plaque for Max Brod on the wall of the New Jewish Cemetery.
Top: The Franz Kafka Monument by Jaroslav Róna.

113

V. Promenading Through Prague

The drawing "Man with a Walking Cane" by Franz Kafka.

Below: Flaneurs on the Rieger quay near Sophie's Island (around 1906).

Bottom right: The Chain Footbridge at today's Mánes Bridge (around 1906).

People taking a walk the old-fashioned way with hat and cane have become a rare sight nowadays. Franz Kafka was that type of passionate walker, his diaries are peppered with reports of outings, city excursions, and jaunts through the streets of Prague, which in some cases extended over several hours. Until the time he fell seriously ill Kafka could walk interminably, often alone, but frequently also in the company of friends or family. Nothing tired him out, "while walking back then I never reached the limits of strength". When relatives came to visit and the apartment reverberated with noise, Kafka retired "unseen, unheard through the front room" and went for a walk through Prague's many lanes. On his walks he could make observations and indulge in reflections on his literary activity: "Walked for two hours through the streets, weightless, boneless, bodiless, and contemplated on what I had withstood while writing this afternoon." Kafka was wont to write postcards to people on his walks as if he had taken a journey: "The very first wishes for a good morning. I'm just preparing for a huge walk, the likes of which I can't remember having taken for weeks. Perhaps it will take an hour. Then I will also make the effort to stroll up and down this Alchemist's Lane once, as it is depicted here on this card."

One of Kafka's preferred routes led him along the quay of the Moldau to the Hetzinsel (Hunt Island), an expansive island in the river on which nobles hunted and coursed until 1802 and where, in Kafka's times, shaded promenades and simple garden taverns awaited visitors. The quay facilities, new at that time, served not only shipping traffic on

114

the river but also kept the flood waters back from the Old Town. Around the turn of the century they had become popular promenades, giving good views of the wide river and its bends, the wooded islands, the mighty bridges, and the sea of houses extending out on both banks. Kafka often embarked on evening walks, in the years 1911 and 1912 with Yitzhak Löwy in particular. On Christmas Eve 1911, Kafka set out with Löwy on a walk "toward Stern", meaning the Renaissance "Star" summer palace and the zoological garden of the same name. Both are close to the site of the Battle of White Mountain, so fateful for Bohemian history. Had the two friends really walked to the Star palace, it would have been equivalent to many hours' hiking. But perhaps the two ramblers decided to take the tramway up to Střeschowitz and walked from there to Stern palace in less than an hour.

Kafka frequently walked over to the Lesser Town, which could be reached in a few minutes by crossing the Charles Bridge or the Kettensteg; the latter was a chain footbridge constructed in the years 1868/69, spanning the Moldau River until 1914. The short route over to the Lesser Town led via the following waypoints: "Across the quay, stone bridge, short stretch in the Lesser Town, new bridge, home. Exciting statues of saints on the Charles Bridge. The curious evening light of summer while the bridge is in its nocturnal emptiness." "New bridge" meant the Svatopluk Čech Bridge, which had been opened to traffic in 1908.

From the Lesser Town Kafka could climb the Laurenziberg (Mount St Lawrence), a forested hill with an observation tower built in 1891 along the lines of the Eiffel Tower in Paris, a church consecrated to Saint Lawrence, an entertaining cabinet of mirrors, and a series of further attractions. The footpath led up by way of the Welsche Gasse (Italian Street), past the Lobkowicz Palace, and finally up approximately 260 stone steps shaded by leafy branches to the observation tower. Access to these grounds was also possible

Walk with Löwy down by the river. One particular pillar of the arch rising up from the Elizabeth Bridge illuminated on the inside by electric light – a dark mass between light streaming out on either side – looked like the chimney of a factory, the dark wedge of a shadow spreading out from it like ascending smoke. The sharply defined green light surfaces at the side of the bridge.

Diary entry by Kafka on December 14, 1911

115

Afterwards walk with Ottla, Miss Taussig, Mr and Mrs Baum, and Pick, Elizabeth Bridge, Quay, Kleinseite, Café Radetzky, Stone Bridge, Charles Street. I still had a glimpse of my earlier good mood, so that one couldn't be too put out with me at the moment.

Diary entry by Kafka on March 3, 1912

Neruda Lane (1906).

from the Aujezd Street, either via well kept walkways that wend their way up in a serpentine path or by means of a cable car, the "lanovka", which is still in use today. On the evening of May 18, 1910, the eagerly awaited "night of the comet", Kafka climbed up the Laurenziberg along with Max Brod, Franz Blei, and the latter's wife and son in order to view Halley's Comet, which was due to approach very near to earth between four and five o'clock in the morning.

The path up to the Hradschin (Prague Castle) led through Neruda Lane, as Kafka remarked in December 1911: "Pleasant lonely walk to the Hradschin and through the Belvedere after those parts in R. & S. ["Richard and Samuel"] turned out well. In Neruda Lane, a plaque: Anna Křižová, seamstress, trained in France by the widowed Duchess Ahrenberg née Princess Ahrenberg. – I stood in the middle of the first castle courtyard and watched the castle guards carry out an alarm drill."

In the evening hours, too, Kafka liked to take the path up to the old imperial castle. In his thoughts he composed letters to his fiancée Felice when he went on long, lonely walks in the cold, "back and forth through the city, via the Hradschin, all around the cathedral, and back through the Belvedere". Or another time: "Coincidentally I took the opposite direction to my usual way, namely the chain footbridge, Hradschin, Charles Bridge. Other times I literally fall down on this path, today coming from the opposite direction I raised myself up a bit."

Particularly popular with passionate walkers were the garden and park facilities of the Belvedere Heights (Letná), which had a magnificent view and on which stretched the so-called Crown Prince Rudolf Grounds. From the Belvedere Heights it was only a few hundred meters further to one of the most popular excursion destinations for people living in Prague, the Royal Arboretum (Königlicher Baumgarten) with avenues, park benches, meadows, and well-kept promenades. This former zoological garden was one of the most charming park facilities in all of central Europe after it was laid out in its present form at the beginning of the 19th century. As soon as the weather allowed, elegant Prague society met in the well-managed café-restaurant or amused itself at picnics and jaunty open air concerts. The gentlemen enjoyed watching the pretty ladies and girls wearing enormous hats with ostrich feathers or wide-brimmed straw hats, sitting on park benches or on quilted blankets under the shadow of exotic trees. During Kafka's time the trees, of which there were over one hundred different species, were still labeled with little plaques giving their Latin, Czech, and German names.

"Friday at the Arboretum": Detail from an oil painting by Viktor Barvitius (1865).

The eastern end of the park was the site of the Regional Anniversary Exposition in 1891. The halls and pavilions erected then are still used for exhibitions today. There was also a gallery for modern art with works by contemporary Czech and German Bohemian artists: "Monday, a public holiday, in the Arboretum, in the restaurant, in the gallery. Sorrow and joy, guilt and innocence like the fingers of two hands inextricably intertwined in one another, one would have to cut through them, through flesh, blood, and bones."

Reporting on a walk he had taken with Ottla and a cousin in April 1914, Kafka declared to his fiancée Felice that he had always only thought of her: "during the whole walk, in the electric streetcar, in the Arboretum, at the pond, listening to the open air concert, eating bread and butter (I even ate a bite of bread and butter in the afternoon, one monstrosity after the

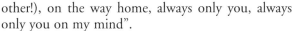

The pleasure with which I sat in the Chotek Gardens yesterday and on the Charles Square reading Strindberg's 'On the Open Sea'.

Diary entry by Kafka on March 23, 1915

Below: Gentleman and lady at the horse races in Kuchelbad near Prague (around 1909).

Right: The Prague Municipal Park with the Franz Joseph Train Station in the background (1900).

other!), on the way home, always only you, always only you on my mind".

Among the most favored destinations of his walks through Prague was the quiet Chotek Park behind the Belvedere Palace, where a romantic statue memorializes the Czech poet Julius Zeyer. From Kafka's diary notes of November 1914 we learn: "Today a partially nice Sunday. Read Dostoyevsky's letter of defense in the Chotek Gardens. The guards on watch duty at the palace and at the corps command. The fountain in the Thun Palace." Or in March 1915: "Sat in the Chotek Gardens. The nicest spot in Prague, birds were singing, the palace with the gallery, the old trees with last year's foliage still dangling from them, the semi-darkness. Later Ottla came with D. [Josef David]."

The area behind Prague Castle, still overgrown with trees during Kafka's childhood and used as drill grounds at most, was built up at the turn of the century. First came new, spacious, and comfortable barracks built north of the "Marienschanze", an old redoubt in the castle district. They housed cadet schools for a k. u. k. infantry regiment and a supply chain regiment. Then the bastions and the area in front of the defense fortifications were turned into expensive building plots and today's Badeni Street (Badeniho) and At-the-Ramparts (Na Valech) were laid out. In June 1913, Kafka wrote to his lover Felice in Berlin about the new buildings in the area, "where, according to my dreams, we should live together." To put some weight behind these proposals, Kafka put down 500 crowns for shares in a "cooperative for the erection of houses for civil servants". After the inglorious end to his engagement with Felice, however,

Kafka's need for a family flat had dwindled down somewhat. Moreover, the World War looming on the horizon in summer 1914 put paid to any dreams of flat-ownership.

At the turn of the 20th century, Prague's Municipal Park (Prager Stadtpark) was an elegant urban garden with monuments, shady trees, flower beds, well-kept lawns, and a broad avenue which divided the park lengthways. One of its particular ornaments was a pond with an island and an artificial waterfall cascading over mighty stone blocks. The residences of Prague's patricians surrounded the park, among them the parental home of Franz Werfel. Today, the grounds once occupied by the park have been almost completely gobbled up by the multiple lanes of a city highway and additions to the railway station. Likewise, the upper-middle class inhabitants of the area, who had settled in its immediate vicinity before the First World War, have all but disappeared.

Complete futility. Sunday. At night particular insomnia. Until ¼ past 11 in bed with the sun shining. Walk. Lunch. Reading the newspaper, leafing through old catalogues. Walk Hybernergasse, Municipal Park, Wenceslas Square, Ferdinandstraße, then toward Podol. Extended it with great effort to 2 hours.

Diary entry by Kafka on November 21, 1915

CONTENTS:

KAFKA-SITES IN PRAGUE:

© Vitalis, s.r.o., Praha 2010 • Translated from the German by Anthony Northey • Printed and bound in the European Union • ISBN 978-80-7253-303-9 • All rights reserved • www.vitalis-verlag.com

SOURCES:

The book in hand is an abridged version of Harald Salfellner's *Franz Kafka and Prague* (2007, ISBN 978-80-7253-214-8). For detailed bibliographic information please refer to the latter edition.

Unless stated otherwise, the illustrations in this book have been taken from the publisher's archive of historical images and publications.

Hartmut Binder Archive, Ditzingen: Page 3 top, 3 bottom, 4 bottom, 5 top, 6, 8, 10–11 top, 14 top, 17 top, 23, 24 top, 24 top, 25, 31 top, 34, 36 top, 36 bottom, 37, 39, 41, 44, 54, 56, 61, 63, 64, 65, 66, 67, 69 right, 90, 91, 92, 98 middle row / left, 98 middle row / right, 104, 109 bottom
Štenc Archive, Prague: Page 111
Bodleian Library, Oxford: Page 59 top
Austrian National Library, Vienna / ANNO: *Prager Tagblatt:* Page 16, 18, 20 bottom, 53, 68, 79, 80 top, 81 bottom, 83 top

Jürgen Born et al.: *Franz Kafka. Kritik und Rezeption 1924–1938* (1983): Page 72 top, 95 bottom
Jürgen Born et al.: *Franz Kafka. Kritik und Rezeption zu seinen Lebzeiten 1912–1924* (1979): Page 106 top
Gustav Janouch: *Franz Kafka und seine Welt* (1965): Page 32, 71 bottom, 83 bottom
Pavel Scheuffler: *Krásné časy* (1995): Page 9, 118
Hugo Siebenschein: *Franz Kafka a Praha* (1947): Page 4 top, 22, 100, 112 top
Rainer Stach: *Die Jahre der Entscheidungen* (2002): Page 70
Tomáš Vrbka: *Státní opera Praha* (2004): Page 76